Shadowspell Academy

THE CULLING TRIALS

BOOK 1

K.F. BREENE

SHANNON MAYER

Contact info:
www.kfbreene.com
books@kfbreene.com

www.shannonmayer.com
shannonmayerauthor@gmail.com

ALSO BY K.F. BREENE

DEMON DAYS VAMPIRE NIGHTS WORLD

Born in Fire

Raised in Fire

Fused in Fire

Natural Witch

Natural Mage

Natural Dual-Mage

www.kfbreene.com

ALSO BY SHANNON MAYER

DESERT CURSED SERIES

Witch's Reign

Dragon's Ground

Jinn's Dominion

Oracle's Haunt

www.shannonmayer.com

Chapter 1

"Damn it, Wild, hold her tight or she's going to gore me!"

"Easier said…than done…old man…" I labored to hold on as Bluebell, our fifteen-hundred-pound longhorn, tried to swing her great head around and get a look at my dad, who was sewing up a gaping hole in her side. She'd had a run in with Whiskers, our massive bull, unfortunately named by my sister when she was younger. Whiskers wasn't known for being easy on the ladies. He was probably still pissed about the name. "She's in a really…*really*…" I flexed my hands around the smooth horn, cursing under my breath as my fingers slid closer to the tip. "Bad mood!"

I barely heard him huff out a laugh.

I gritted my teeth and dug my heels into the loose soil, pushing against the metal of our makeshift chute for leverage. The ramshackle affair groaned and crackled. Bluebell stomped her foot in impatience or maybe pain, and a splatter of mud flew up and slapped my face. The glop of rank-smelling muck slid over the corner of my mouth and infiltrated my lips before I could close them. I fought not to gag, settled for spitting to the side and tried not to taste what had just landed on my tongue.

Much as I loved being a farm girl, moments like these made me wish for a house in the city. Houston. Dallas. Anywhere in Texas but the great nowhere I called home, a quarter mile from the nearest neighbor and a tiny town five miles beyond that. The moment was fleeting, and I spat again, clearing the last of the sludge from my mouth.

That had better *be mud...*

I craned my neck to get a view of my dad.

"Johnson, you good?" I hollered.

His failing body had a harder and harder time keeping up each year, an open secret in our family. A cripple before his time, he couldn't dance out of the way of a pissed off cow like he once had. Dad was in his mid-forties, but moved as if he were a hundred plus. But his hands were still steadier than anyone's, though, when it came to stitching up the animals... assuming I could keep the cow's big butts in our crappy cow chute, of course, something I wasn't excelling at in that moment.

"Good," he called out, strain in his voice. "Just slow going. Thick hide on our ol' Bluebell, you know."

Bluebell jerked to the side, dragging my feet through the mud. With a growl and a heave, I yanked her back to nearly straight and held on. The chute groaned and the weld closest to me began to open. If it broke free, we'd be wrestling with Bluebell in a whole new arena.

"Come on, you fat cow, stop fighting!" I growled, as frustrated as a woodpecker on an iron post.

She let out a bellow and jerked her head toward him again. My knee bashed into the metal panel and I yelped, barely keeping my grip on her horn. Bluebell shifted gears fast, slamming her shoulder into the panel and using it as leverage. Damn it, smart cows were going to be the end of me. The other end of the panel swung out and smacked my dad, sending him flying.

He yelled, and there was the distinct sound of a body hitting the mud.

I'm sure he hoped it was mud, at any rate.

"Tell me you didn't break your neck!" I called out, breathing hard and pushing aside a sudden spike of anxiety. My knee throbbed, but I barely felt it over the worry. "Dad?"

There was a good five seconds that felt like a heck of a lot longer where he didn't answer.

"I'm fine," he grunt-laughed, and I let out a breath I didn't know I'd been holding. His dark hair and ballcap slowly appeared above the cow's shoulder again. "I didn't see that one coming. One day, we'll get a proper chute. One of those big head gates maybe."

"We sure will. Just gotta start playing that lotto."

"I keep telling you to get a ticket. With your luck, all our problems would be over."

I laughed and pulled on Bluebell's horn again, adjusting my grip. If only that were true, I'd scrounge up a few bucks and make the long trek into town tomorrow for a stack of tickets. Sadly, it was my older brother, Tommy, who'd always been the lucky one. Whole lot of good it had done him in the end.

A black cloud settled over me at that wayward thought, and grief, old but still raw, churned in my gut like soured milk. I shook my head to dislodge the heavy pallor and forced myself to focus on the task at hand. What had happened to Tommy was in the past. Too late to change it.

I bent my head and wiped the sweat from my face onto my upper arm. The end of summer in Texas was as hot as the devil's thong and about as humid. The rain the night before hadn't been any help to us.

"Stop daydreaming, Johnson," I said, a little too seriously. My hands slid farther, sweat making them slick. "I can't hold her much longer."

You'd think that after losing his wife and oldest son long before their times, my dad's outlook on life in general would have dimmed. No, that pessimism was left to me. I no longer even had my best childhood friend to help carry the load. At least Rory, the kid I'd grown up with, had found a better life. He still had a future, unlike Mom and Tommy.

I just wished he hadn't forgotten me so completely.

"Almost got it done, Wild, just two more stitches," Dad said.

I breathed slowly, my muscles spazzing after holding Bluebell's horn for so long. "Fat head," I grumbled at her. "You're lucky one of us likes you."

She let out a long, low moo, rolled her eye closest to me, and I relaxed my hand, thinking she was calming down.

Big mistake.

As soon as I let off the pressure, Bluebell jerked her head to the side, and my fingers slid to the tip of the horn. "Dad, I can't hold her!"

He couldn't move fast enough; I knew it. I clutched with my fingernails, my upper body shaking with effort, nails digging in as I snarled with the effort.

"Hurry!"

Dad limped away from Bluebell, hunched over, but two steps were enough to put him out of her range. I let go of her and she whipped her head to the side, her horns ripping through the space where he'd been standing only a moment before.

I backed up and bent at the waist, hands on my knees

as I blew out a few deep breaths. My body trembled from my shoulders down to my calves. I was going to be sore in the morning.

Who needed the gym when you had to wrestle with cows on a regular basis?

"Good job, Wild. I finished up that last stitch. Keep her and that calf of hers separate from the others for a few days before letting them back in with the rest of the herd." Dad spoke over his shoulder, his instructions given in a pain-filled voice as he limped toward the house.

I understood why. If he stopped to talk, he might not get going again. The last time, I'd had to carry him into the house. It had been more than humiliating for him. What father wanted his teenage daughter to care for him like that? Certainly not a Texan, a rough neck, born and bred.

"Got it." I stood upright and stretched my hands over my head, my back cracking with a long series of pops that sent a shiver down my spine. I patted Bluebell on the forehead and scratched her behind one ear. "You're a turd, you know that? The man was just trying to help you."

She mooed at me and licked my jeans like nothing more than an oversized dog, her horns carefully kept away from me now that she wasn't being restrained.

"Total turd," I muttered as I checked to make sure my

dad was out of the small corral before I let her loose. She'd go for him, even now that he wasn't bothering her. He was basically the vet around here, and she didn't like going to the doctor.

I watched as he slipped through the main gate and latched it behind him. He didn't talk about what ailed him, just called it *The Sickness,* as if that meant something. And honestly, it must've. At least to my mother when she was alive. But to the kids, no explanation was given, and if we asked, we were punished, or he'd just shrug and walk away. We didn't think he'd outlive our mother. But life has a way of randomly kicking you in the gut. My family got kicked more often than most.

I chewed my lip as I looked out over our sprawling ranch. Dad's optimism couldn't change the fact that our bills kept mounting while our revenue slowly decreased—only money would do that. Maybe I *should* start playing the lotto. Couldn't hurt at this point and it wasn't like the few dollars a week I'd spend would save us in the end any other way.

I sighed and unlatched our makeshift chute, letting Bluebell into the small corral.

"There you go, turd," I muttered, patting her hip as she went by.

She mooed softly at her six-month-old calf, who'd hid in the corner of the corral while we worked, and he ran over to her, rubbing against her head as she licked him all over.

I worked to get two of the panels unlatched and lifted them, balancing them on my shoulder, and then carefully made my way to the side of the corral to stack them with the others.

"What a waste of a life."

I startled at the unfamiliar voice, and turned slowly, seeing a solid man with a crew cut and aviators leaning against the fence. I hadn't heard the crunch of tires on gravel.

A glance behind him, then a sweep with my gaze, told me why—he didn't have a car. Or at least not one within sight.

I frowned. Strangers out this way were rare, but walking strangers rarer still, especially if they didn't have one holy book or another clutched between their palms.

Stalling for time, I headed to grab another panel, assessing him while I did so. He was five foot eight or nine, a few inches shorter than me, with a lean body poised in such a way that there was no mistaking the loosely contained power coiled within him. He reminded me of the mountain lions that occasionally came through the farm. Even when they were still, you could see the potential in them to launch at you with the blink of an eye. Sideburns crawled down his square face, otherwise clean of stubble.

Although his clothing was dark and non-descript, he wore a patch on his right shoulder, the symbol done up with red lines in a series of angles. At this distance, I couldn't make out the details, but even still, a memory floated up out of the darkness. A patch on one of my mom's old jackets.

Web of Wryd.

"Girl," the man said, clearly short on patience.

"I'm eighteen, mister," I said before I dropped the panel. Metal clanged, giving me a moment to turn. "Call me *woman.* Or lady, if you're interested in a fat lip."

He stared at me across the space, and the push of his focus nearly made me step back. Cold shivers worked up my spine, everything in my body screaming *danger!*

"Derelict, then," he said. Our versions of compromise didn't line up too well, but he didn't give me time to say so. "Where is the boy?"

"Didn't take to the vocabulary lessons in school, huh?" I took two slow steps, outwardly loose and relaxed, and leaned an elbow against the nearest fence. I didn't trust the raging energy I felt pulsing from him, even from the distance. It spoke of a predator, and if I spooked, that would make me the prey. I didn't know much about people, but I knew a great deal about animals—he was not someone to turn your back on and live.

"The boy has been summoned," the man said. "I must

speak with him."

"Can't. He's not home from school." I checked my watch. "He'll be getting loaded up on the bus. I wouldn't mess with the bus driver, Ms. Everdeen, though. She isn't allowed to smoke during her school run, and it makes her so cranky, she grows horns to hold up her halo."

The stranger's lips pulled to the side in a smirk, and he minutely shook his head. "It's a pity you elected not to go to school. You're a natural."

He took a step back and I couldn't help a confused frown. I didn't have the money for college, but why should he care? Is that what he'd meant about a waste of a life? Because when you were flat broke, and your family depended on you to survive, staying on the farm was a matter of necessity.

"See that the boy gets the envelope," the stranger said, walking toward the long driveway. "I'll be around later to discuss the particulars."

"What you really need is to discuss those sideburns with a barber," I mumbled, watching him silently make his way along the fence.

I blinked and swept my gaze out over the farm. A pang of regret hit me thinking about college. All kids dreamed about what they wanted to be when they grew up, and I hadn't been the exception. I'd never thought mediocre grades and a penchant to talk back would keep me from setting my footprints on the moon, or becoming a vet, or once, when I'd been in a reall becoming a mortician. And I'd been ri hadn't held me back. My sense of duty ha

Well, that, and a serious lack of funds.

I probably should've tried harder in school. Kept my mouth shut a little more. Then maybe I could've gotten a scholarship like Tommy had. Then again, look how his big break had turned out. His chance at a better life had turned into a death certificate. No, I was better off with the farm. At least I knew the dangers here.

Replaying what the stranger had said, something about the envelope he'd mentioned but neglected to give me twanged my memory banks. A cold sweat popped along my skin and I turned back to the stranger to ask him a question, only to see…nothing.

He was gone.

"No way," I said softly, taking a few steps toward the driveway and road far beyond. The land was flat and cleared—I should've still seen him. Even if he'd started running, he couldn't have disappeared that quickly and I would have heard him on the gravel if he'd sprinted. Yet…there was no sign of him.

A strange tremor worked through my body, the warning of danger taking root. Something wasn't right with that man. He was trouble. I could feel it all the way to the marrow of my bones.

CHAPTER 2

An hour later, after I'd finished the last of the chores outside, I stood in the kitchen of our rundown, termite-ridden, hundred-year-old farmhouse, heart and mind racing, as I stared down at the pock-marked and cracked kitchen table. The clutter that usually choked the surface had been cleared away to Lord knew where. The kitchen counter had been set to rights, everything tucked into cabinets, or maybe the garbage can. The mostly empty canisters of sugar and flour were lined up, nice and tidy.

There was no way my father had done this, not with the knocks he'd taken in the pasture. The twins wouldn't have bothered even if they were home.

A hefty manila envelope lay in the exact center of the table, and when I saw it, one of the last memories I had of my older brother rushed over me.

"You guys will never believe what I got!" Tommy set the fat manila envelope on the clean kitchen table like it

contained a bar of gold. He stepped back and fist pumped the air. "Guy came up to me and said it was special delivery. It's not mine yet, but, Dad..." he grinned like a maniac, "all our prayers have been answered. This is what we've been waiting for."

"Why?" I inched forward, Tommy's smile infectious. "What is it?"

"It's..." He shook his head and reached forward to gingerly touch the envelope, clearly caught up in the moment and unable to get the words out.

"What?" I chuckled and stood beside him, anticipation filling me.

"An invitation to the trials," my father said softly. "To school, if you pass."

A strange heaviness dragged at my father's words, threads of fear and hope mingled tightly together.

"School?" I asked. "But...I thought we couldn't afford it?"

"That's the thing, Wild." My brother beamed. "The envelope has—"

"No." My father stood and pulled the envelope with him. He pinched the flap closed. "No, Thomas. You are not to discuss the contents of the envelope with anyone but me. Your mother..." My father's jaw set in that stubborn way I knew from when my mother was alive. He hadn't said no

to her often, but occasionally, when she tried to enforce something he didn't agree with, he'd dig in his heels as hard as any of the thick-headed longhorns in the pasture. I wondered what in that envelope had set him off.

"We'll talk about it, Thomas, just you and me," he said, turning away. "We'll see what they have to say. I'd hate to pass up an opportunity because of old superstitions."

Tommy shrugged at me, as confused as I was, apparently, his eyes glittering with excitement before he followed Dad from the room.

Three years later, I stared down at an identical manila envelope, curiosity eating away at me. Just like before, there was nothing written on the envelope, no name, no *do not open*, but I knew. This envelope was for my little brother, Billy. The stranger had asked for him by gender if not by name. And even if he hadn't, I would have known anyway, as certainly as I'd known my father would let Tommy run off to that prestigious college.

Whoever had sent both envelopes was trying to poach the boys of this family, one by one.

This time, though, I had the power to stop it.

"Dad?" I called, still staring at that envelope like I might a hornet trapped in an outhouse with me.

"In here, Wild," he called from the living room, easy

to hear in our small house. "I'm just taking a break for a minute."

"Did you hear anyone in here earlier?" I asked, my hands shaking.

"Do you mean the twins?" He paused. "Isn't it early for them to be home?"

I shook my head, frustration eating at me. First, the stranger had shown up without my noticing, then he'd vanished on the way to the driveaway, and now this? Why had he cleaned my kitchen, and how had he done it quietly enough not to bother Dad?

"Dad, you need anything?" I yelled louder than needed.

"No, Wild, I'm good. I'll just take another minute, if you don't need me."

That minute would last the next few days if he held to the usual pattern of recuperation. My old man was too proud to call it like it was.

"It's fine, Dad."

I snatched up that envelope and reached for the knife hanging at my belt. What I knew of the school was very little. My brother had passed the trials, whatever those were, and been admitted into the academy. My father had been ecstatic in one beat and strangely guilt-ridden the next.

Tommy had thrived in his first year, jumping to top

in his class (like always). He'd had whatever my dad lacked—according to my dad's mumbling one night after a few glasses of celebratory Scotch. All was going great…until, without warning, our lives were turned upside down.

A notice was left on our doorstep that Tommy had died in a freak accident. The details were classified, they'd said, although no one cared to explain why. When my father pressed, he was stonewalled. Ignored like a stranger. They didn't even send Tommy's body home. Sure, they'd sent a pine box, but it had been empty. For some reason, my father didn't raise a fuss about that. When I pleaded with him, he cut me off in much the same way he would when asked about *The Sickness.* The topic was closed for discussion. End of story.

No one from the school had attended the funeral. We'd received no condolences. Hell, even Rory, our lifelong family friend—nearly a brother, we were so close—hadn't bothered to come home. Hell, maybe he didn't know. The only address I had for him was from a postcard he'd sent. We were alone in our grief, in the dark about the cause and completely powerless to do anything about any of it.

After the funeral, my father never mentioned the school again. He'd kept on hoping for a better life, acting as though someone would ride in and rescue us. As though something might come of all his dreaming. Which had left me to carry the weight of Tommy's loss these last two years.

And here we were again. This accursed envelope. This death threat tolling Billy's name.

The heavily worn handle of my knife, made from a longhorn, was comfortable against my palm. My parents had made it for me ages ago, back when I was starting to help out on the land. Back when the family had been whole and happy.

Back before freak accidents like the one that had taken my mother, and phantom schools that didn't allow an investigation or offer an explanation when one of their students died mysteriously. Back when life had been good.

I slipped the gleaming edge into the opening. I slid it through the top of the envelope, the paper cutting clean with a sharp tearing sound.

A deep breath and my knife firmly in my hand in case something nasty fell out, I grabbed a corner and dumped the contents of the envelope onto the worn wood. Metal trinkets clattered across the table, followed by a silver envelope and gleaming new smart watch. Finally, a wad of cash bound with a thick rubber band. The bill on top made my eyes widen. A quick flip through the stack and I could barely breathe.

Hundred dollar bills. All of them.

No wonder my brother had nearly peed himself with excitement when he'd gotten his envelope.

My lip curled in distaste.

They intended to bribe my younger brother in the same way. To entice him to his death, just like Tommy.

Fat freaking chance.

Memories filtered through my mind, unbidden. The Costco run that had filled our pantry, cabinets, and storehouse with staples that would last for the year. The clothes my brother had claimed Rory had helped him steal from a big store in Dallas. I remembered Dad muttering about a gift horse and the full-ride scholarship, cloaked in guilt while simultaneously beaming in pride.

I hadn't really understood the conflicting emotions rolling off our father in waves. At fifteen, I hadn't had the wind knocked out of me yet. The twins had been old enough to enjoy the windfall of good fortune but too young to make sense of it.

Finally, one last memory filtered through as I stood in front of more money than I'd seen in my entire life.

Tommy, Rory, and I had been sitting underneath the weeping willow at the far end of the acreage on a sweltering late summer day, not unlike today. Tommy was supposed to leave for the academy the following morning, and this was our last goodbye. Rory had leaned forward to look Tommy square in the eyes and said, "Never trust someone that throws money at you, Tank. People like that have more money than sense, and more sense than morals. Think fast, and make friends slow, or not at all."

It had been good advice. Advice Rory was probably following, wherever he was.

A familiar sadness washed over me. A year after Tommy left, Rory had headed out west without even a proper goodbye. He'd stuck a note to the outside of my window, the way he'd done for years, only this one wasn't "meet me in the apple orchard" or "I found a stack of fireworks." This one had crushed me.

"Off to the West Coast. Chasing dreams. Be safe, Wild." That was all it had said, signed as always with the slash of an R. Aside from an occasional postcard, I hadn't heard from him since. Clearly, he'd moved on from this nowhere town and his hard life.

I heaved a sigh. At least he was alive. He'd better have been, at any rate, though his dad would never let us know if something had happened.

I lowered myself onto the chair in our kitchen, the contents of the envelope spread around me, and leaned my elbows heavily on the table. Then, unable to help myself, I set my hand up beside the stack of money for a quick measurement. Just over four inches or so.

I thought back to Tommy's first year at the academy. To the windfall that had given us a year's worth of supplies, clothes, and improvements. Given what I knew of finances from my few years of handling the farm without much help, I could only guess how much money sat in that stack. All told, it had to be nearly forty grand. Maybe more, but I'd have to count it and I didn't have time for that before the twins got home.

As if my thoughts had summoned it, the clock above the kitchen door chimed three times and I jumped. I let my breath out slowly, trying to calm my nerves. Three already? I was way behind.

With shaking hands I tried to ignore, I grabbed the watch and a shiver rolled over me, cold air whispering up my arm to my shoulder. I shoved it into the envelope, followed by the money that threatened to cling to my hand. Everything inside, I rushed the whole package upstairs to my room on the third floor, the only room up there. I needed to talk to my dad about all this, alone, and with the twins due home any minute, now wasn't the time. It would have to wait until tonight.

A loose floorboard under my bed used to be my favorite stashing spot, but the twins and my dad knew it and they regularly snooped to see if I'd put aside any good chocolate. I did a slow turn. My room wasn't big and I didn't have a lot of choices.

"Closet," I said and shoved the package into an old backpack. That would have to do for now.

Ten seconds later, the thundering of feet on the floorboards downstairs, followed by a stampede up the stairs, announced the twins' arrival.

"Slow down before you bust a plank!" I yelled from my room.

"Hey!" Sam stuck her head into my room, wild red curls spilling in every direction as if they were a living creature on her head. "What's for dinner?"

I shook my own head, a few dark strands loosening from my ponytail, and hurried toward the door, brushing past her. "I don't know. It's been a busy day."

Billy met me on the stairs as I headed down, his hands lifted in the air, shock written all over his face. "What do you mean, *you don't know*?"

"I'm leaving it up to my first and finest cooking pupils." I put my hand on the wall to scoot around him, jumping over the last step that was dodgy on the best of days. It needed to be replaced—I just hadn't gotten around to it.

"You're teaching people to cook?" Billy ran down after me, stopping in the kitchen doorway. "But you're not any good at it. How can you teach anything other than how not to burn stuff?"

"Then I look forward to the students outperforming

the master. Step right up, you heathens, and let's learn some stuff!"

Billy's eyes widened as understanding dawned. "I have homework," he shouted, backing away. "Lots of homework. Summer school is really all about the homework."

"I do too," Sam said, crashing into Billy's back before she could stop herself. "And chores."

"And chores!" Billy chorused.

I grinned as I grabbed a pan out of the cabinet.

"Are you sure you don't want to help me? You can plan the whole menu if you do." I turned my back so I could school my features. If they knew I was upset, they'd start asking questions. As it was, they were always on high alert for the next bad thing to happen. I couldn't blame them really. At nearly sixteen, they'd experienced more heartache and loss than most middle-aged people. "Just think, you could plan out the entire week ahead of time, so you'd always know what would be for dinner. What a relief that would be, huh?"

Billy scratched his head, his unruly hair as dark as Sam's was red. They might have been twins but they couldn't have been more opposite. "I think I'd rather a surprise every night."

"I'd much rather a surprise," Sam agreed with him, ganging up on me yet again. "Wild, listen to this. Remember that boy—"

"Jaaaaysus, not this again," Billy drawled, and I promptly forced out a laugh. Another day, I would have laughed for real.

Sam frowned and then her hand shot out, a mere blur as she smacked him upside the head. "At least I can talk to my crush face-to-face. All you've seen of Miss Gothic lady what's-her-face is a few pics and words on a screen! How's that chat group, anyway, grandpa?"

Billy's face turned red. "You're just jealous that I have more Facebook friends than you do."

"Facebook is for old people."

"I wish I had a phone instead of that crappy ol' library computer so I could do Snapchat," Billy muttered.

I twisted my lips to the side in unease, wishing I could buy them flashy new devices—or even an old used one. We didn't have any cellphones or computers to our name—we couldn't afford it. Anything online needed to be done at the library or the high school, including their social media presences, something I didn't even have. Not that it mattered. I had no friends anymore to hook up with.

"I'm going to marry that boy one day," Sam said. "He's going to be your brother-in-law." She lifted her nose and stared down it at her twin. A dare for him to speak if I ever saw it.

"Marry him tomorrow so I can have your room too." Billy grinned as he swiped an apple off the counter.

"She'd probably ask to move him in here, then you'd be out of a room altogether," I said, badgering him.

Sam's scowl deepened until I wasn't even sure her eyes were open. They paused for a moment, like two cats eyeing each other up, and then they tore out of the house, Billy leading, Sam close behind, screaming at him not to be a jackass.

"Language!" I yelled after them, not that it did any good, or that I ever expected it to. But Mom had attempted to raise us as well-behaved, softly spoken, non-swearing children, and she'd want me to take up her mantle.

I was doing a terrible job. But then, she'd done a terrible job, too, if I was any proof.

Reality seeped back in and my grin slid from my face. I leaned against the counter. I had to focus on one thing at a time. Dinner. I had to get dinner ready. We didn't have much, but we had livestock and a few green thumbs between us. We'd put one of the older cows—Annabelle—in the freezer the month before, which meant we ate better than most this far below the poverty line.

I cooked on autopilot as my mind worked over just what I was going to do.

"Dad?" I called as I flipped the steaks in the frying

pan with the dip in the middle. With the twins out of the house doing their afternoon chores, this would be a good time to talk to him alone. Maybe the only time before he turned in early as was his nightly schedule.

"Yeah, Wild?" he called back in a thick voice. I knew full well he was napping, another routine part of our days, but this couldn't wait.

I moved the steaks off the heat and washed my hands quickly before snagging a tea towel to dry them. I wound the towel around my hands, worrying the material as I walked to the TV room at the front of the house.

Dad was leaned back in his recliner, legs propped by a cushion, his head supported by a pillow. "I was just going to get up," he murmured, his eyes at half mast, but he didn't make a move. The lie was one he told often enough that we all just acted like it was truth.

I swallowed and nodded. Crap, this was harder than I'd thought it would be.

"You going to strangle me with that?" He lifted a trembling finger and pointed at the tea towel I'd stretched between my hands.

"I'll wait until your back is turned. It's easier that way." I grinned to complement the joke but knew it didn't reach my eyes. I took a breath and dove in. "Listen, I was thinking 'bout Tommy. Thinking about that scholarship—"

"No, we don't talk about that," he said.

"We have to," I said softly. He wasn't the only one hurt by the loss of Tommy, so I tread lightly. "I know you don't want to, Dad, but we have to. I'm not a child any longer." The urge to take his hand swept over me and I pushed it away. Not because I didn't care, but because of the tension in his frame. He did not want to tell me what had happened.

"Why now?" He frowned. "Why do you say we have to?"

"Can you trust me? Just tell me what happened to Tommy, about how the scholarship worked."

I thought his face paled, but he shook it off. "I'm not supposed to talk about it, Wild. Not just because I don't want to relive it." He rubbed a hand over his face and a good minute went by before he spoke again.

"All right, I'll tell you what I can." Dad swallowed hard and the tension in him went from caged fear to pain in a split second. "I should never have let him go," my dad whispered, the grief in his voice like an arrow straight through me. He closed his eyes. "Your mother was right all along, God rest her soul. I was blinded by pride and hope. That was the worst decision I've ever made. Believing he would be safe. That he'd be the one to defeat the system."

My heart beat faster. My father had known Tommy

would be in danger?

"Did…did he get money for going?" I asked, wanting to be sure. "And a watch, and a few…trinkets?"

"Money wasn't worth his life. Money wasn't worth losing him. But it wasn't just the money. It was vanity, Wild. My boy was offered something I'd only ever dreamed of… I wanted to live through him." His dark eyes pleaded with me in the dim light of the room. "I wanted him to be more than his old, broken man. More than this crippled sack of bones. I wondered if he'd be like his mother. If he'd wield that kind of power. She was so damn majestic. I hated that she had to give it up because of a rumor about that curse. Because of the bleating of an—"

His lips thinned and he shook his head again, deflating. "But she was right all along. If I'd only listened to her. If I'd only acted on what she'd made me promise, Thomas would be safe. We'd still have him here, safe with us."

I stared with my mouth open, feeling the depth underlying his words, like standing on an iceberg and wondering how much of it existed below the surface. Even though he was saying more than he'd ever said about the situation with Tommy, so much of his speech didn't make sense.

"What if another envelope came?" I asked softly,

knowing what he'd say.

Or so I thought. My father surprised me.

"I expected it before now," he said, his tone resolute. "Your mother felt the power in you from day one, Wild. From your first cry. Your strength only ever blossomed. It didn't have peaks and valleys, like the others. It only ever grew. She wanted to hide you, most of all. And she tried. Her friend used her blood to cast this place into the shadows. But the blood magic faded after her accident. As soon as they came for Tommy, I knew you'd be next. It was only a matter of time."

Blood magic. Spells. Power. His words sent shivers through me, fear and…excitement. Then his meaning finally sunk in.

I surely looked like a big-mouthed bass standing there, jaw hanging open wide.

"Me? There's power in me?" I asked, dumbfounded. Mom had told us bedtime stories about magic, but that's all they were—stories. Had Dad's sickness addled his brain?

He ignored my question. "Did he come?"

I worked to catch up to him while my brain struggled to make sense of his words. "Who, sideburns guy?"

"Did someone come with an envelope?"

"Yes, but—"

Dad shook his head, slowly. "No, Wild. No buts. We

will not speak with him. You saw what happened to Tommy. It's too dangerous. Tommy was a target, and you will be, too, even more so than your brother. Your mother left that place to stay safe. You'll stay away for the same reason."

I couldn't wrap my head around what he was saying. They were the kinds of words that threatened to change the shape of all you knew. Questions lined up in my head like little toy soldiers. What place did Mom leave? The same school as Tommy? Why was it dangerous?

"But…" I started.

"No, Wild, and that's final." He cranked up the volume on the TV, his way of ending the conversation. "Give the money back. Give it all back. They won't have another of my children. *They will not*!"

He shifted his gaze to the TV, and I stared at him a moment before I turned and trudged back to the kitchen in a fog, my mind whirling. What did my father mean, "my power continued to grow"? Did he mean physical strength? I was surely much stronger than the average girl, but I'd always attributed that to a hard life dealing with large animals. A girl needed a certain amount of strength to work the farm and keep up with the men.

But what did any of that have to do with a college scholarship that included stacks of cash, fancy watches, and trinkets? And why were Tommy and me targets?

Targets of what?

None of this made any sense, starting with sideburns dude somehow sneaking onto the property. Not to mention that the envelope wasn't even for me. Whatever my father thought he knew, clearly he was mistaken. Except for the fact that he should've said no when Tommy had wanted to go, of course.

Suddenly the guilt I'd seen in Dad all those years made a lot more sense. My mother had somehow known Tommy would get asked to this college, whatever it was, and she'd made my Dad promise not to commit. Only, my father had bent to the excitement, and his own desire to live vicariously through Tommy.

One thought kept niggling at me—why hadn't I gotten an envelope if my father was so sure they'd want me? They'd skipped right over me.

"It's a pity you elected not to go to school. You're a natural."

Sideburns had said that, as though it had been my choice to be passed up. As though I'd rejected the invitation already. Yet…my father would've said if one had already come. Right?

I pushed that from my mind. The past didn't matter. What did matter was the envelope coming for too-young Billy.

It struck me that Sam hadn't gotten one either. Whatever my dad thought, my initial assessment held firm—this college, school, whatever it was, was going after the younger males of this family. They were trying to pick them off.

First things first, I needed to find out the nature of this college.

CHAPTER 3

A COUPLE HOURS later, after I served up dinner and all but force-fed the twins their greens, I slipped into the quiet hush of my room and closed the door. The yellow package was still in my closet, right where I'd stashed it. I grabbed it and unceremoniously dumped the contents onto the bed. Five trinkets spilled out first. They reminded me of something, I couldn't quite put my finger on. Each one was tiny, barely bigger than a quarter, but three dimensional. A knife, a gravestone, a pawprint, a tiny stick, and a blank coin. I rolled them through my fingers, then dropped them back to the bed. No clues there.

I zeroed in on the letter in the shiny silver envelope. If anything held answers, that did; I was sure of it.

A quick slit of the paper with my knife, and I pulled out a piece of thick cardstock with feathered edges. Soft vibrations ran up through my fingers as I touched the card. As I watched in utter confusion, embossed letters etched themselves into the cream-colored paper, dancing and swirling across the expensive paper as they formed words.

"What the hell?"

I angled the card away from the light and leaned in to see better, but upon closer inspection, the words were stationary. My dad's babbling about magic must have set off my imagination. My eyes slid over the message and immediately sweat beaded along my brow and slid down my face, one droplet landing on the paper, next to the words I couldn't un-see. Words that could not have been any worse.

Billy Johnson,

Your presence is requested at the Culling Trials.

You don't choose an Academy.

An Academy chooses you.

Report to the address below within forty-eight hours or your family will die.

Time is ticking.

I stared at the words for a long time, longer than I should have considering the last line, then shook the paper, wondering if the letters would rearrange themselves into a more favorable message. Nothing happened, of course. My eyes had been playing tricks on me earlier.

I turned the paper over and searched the back for a customer service number or an April Fool's note. It was late July, but maybe someone was getting a head start on their tomfoolery. Blankness greeted me, a solid white of nothing.

I squinted at the address listed below the message. Upstate New York somewhere.

Crystal Lake Wild Forest, Roscoe, New York.

The ink glittered, as if the threat to my family were a young girl's art project.

The message seemed preposterous. What college threatened people to show up and learn or else? On what planet was that rational?

The same college that covers up students' deaths.

I gritted my teeth as the message in front of me finally sank in. It almost seemed like I could feel the intent behind the embossed words: You will show up regardless, but if we have to make you, your family will die.

I eyed the watch on the bed, its screen a solid black. They'd even sent their own timekeeper. How thoughtful.

If Tommy had been given a watch, I would've seen it. He would've been too proud not to wear it. He also couldn't have gotten a card with a message like this—there was no way he would've been beaming about his acceptance to a school that would threaten his family.

Right?

Given all the skeletons that had gone dancing around the living room earlier, I wasn't sure of anything anymore. Time to hold Dad's feet to the fire and get the rest of the story.

I took the stairs quickly but with light steps, not wanting to bring the twins out of their rooms. In the living room, I gently shook my dad awake. It appeared he hadn't bothered to head to bed. Another part of our routine. "Dad."

"Hmm?" His eyes fluttered opened and it took a moment for him to focus on the card held three feet from his face. "What is it?"

"Dad, did Tommy get an invitation with that manila envelope he got from that school?" I asked.

"Did…what?" My dad rubbed his eyes and struggled to sit up.

I shook the card a little, drawing his eyes to the glittering message.

"Did Tommy get something like this?" I repeated.

His brows lowered, and the sleep fled from his eyes as they traced the words. "What…? No. Thomas didn't get anything like that. He only got a message about the Culling Trials, not the threat. Is that how they're running things now? The older families must be pushing back.

The Helix family wouldn't stand for this. Wait a minute…is that?" He took the card and held it away from his face so he could see better. "That says Billy's name. It can't be." His hand shook as he stared at me over the top of it, the fear heavy in his eyes.

"Yeah." I took the, now bent, card. "The envelope didn't come for me. It came for Billy."

"But…" My father struggled to get his feet down in the recliner so he could properly sit up. "Billy is still in high school. He isn't ready for college yet."

I fought not to crumple the card in my hand. "I know. And he's not going. What is this place, Dad? How is this even legal? You have to give me some answers. We have to figure out how to stop this."

He sighed and rubbed his temple with a gnarled finger. "Sweet Jesus, this can't be happening. Not again." He held up an empty glass to me. "Bring me another glass of elixir, Wild," he said softly.

Without money to spend on Scotch these days, he had to settle for moonshine, what he liked to call elixir. We had a couple of bottles—a present one of the neighbors had given me for hunting down a lone wolf that had terrorized both of our livestock. Dad rarely drank it, saving it for Christmas and special occasions—or for when life and his pain got too heavy to bear.

"Sure, Dad," I said, then gritted my teeth, refusing to

give in to despair. I'd been taking care of things around here for the last few years. So far, I'd kept us above water...or at least we weren't drowning yet. Whatever it took, we'd find a way around this. Billy would not end up like Tommy.

A flash of yellow snagged my attention when I stepped into the kitchen, and I found myself staring at a second manila folder on the kitchen table.

"Buckets of crud..." My voice drifted away as cold trickled down my spine.

He'd been in here again—the dude with the bad side-burns. Him, or someone like him. We'd all been home, going about our lives, and none of us had noticed a stranger in our midst. He was like a ghost!

"Billy! Sam!" I yelled. The chances were slim to none, but I entertained the faint hope that I was wrong. That they'd brought the envelope home from summer school.

Before they could answer, or even emerge from their room, I rushed to the back door and yanked it open. He should still be out there, although I didn't actually expect to see him.

Early evening blanketed the sweeping fields to the side of our house and settled firmly on the barn off to my left. A deep *moo* drifted through the dense evening and the sound of crickets throbbed in the dying light. I usually loved this time of the day, but now it all seemed tainted by the intruder. As though the serenity was washed through with his danger.

I flicked on the porch light and jogged to the edge of the cracked concrete walkway. I squinted into the deep twilight, just bright enough to reveal one clear boot tread in the still damp dirt. Just one, as though he'd stepped down with the intention that I'd notice his presence…before vanishing again.

"What?" Sam stepped out of the house and into the evening light. I turned back to look at her, hands on her hips and an eyebrow arched. "What's the matter?"

Billy jogged out behind her, his brows pinched. "What's up?"

I spun on my heel and marched toward them. "Did you hear anyone come in?"

They both looked around in confusion, the sass in Sam fading.

"Where?" she asked as I brushed by her. "You mean in the house?"

Well, that was a no.

"Close the door," I barked, worry making me sharper than usual. "Lock it. All the locks."

"What's going on?" Billy asked, hurrying in behind Sam. He didn't wait for an answer before he threw the deadbolt and locked the knob.

"It's happening again." My dad staggered as he

neared the door to the kitchen and put a large-knuckled hand on the door frame to stabilize himself. Sam ran forward to help him, slipping under his free arm. Dad's eyes locked on mine. "Wild, we can't let him go. They'll kill him. Thomas was the top of his class—if he couldn't make it through, Billy surely won't."

"Me?" Billy pointed at his chest. "What did I do? I swear it wasn't me!"

"Guilty conscience," Sam muttered. He scowled at her.

"Stop." I held up my hand. "Just hold on. They're not taking Billy anywhere. Sam, Billy, get to bed."

Billy shook his head. "If this is about me, I have a right—"

I silenced him with a look. "It's *not* about you. It's about *me*. Get on with ya. Both of you. Go to bed. We'll talk about this in the morning."

They hesitated, they knew as well as I did that we didn't talk about things in this house—and I pointed at the staircase.

"Go on, now. Let me talk to Dad for a while. We'll figure this out."

They muttered complaints, but after a stern word from my father, they stomped up the stairs. I waited until their bedroom door slammed before I snatched up the second manila envelope and ripped it open, finding a packet of paper. The five symbols emblazoned across the top in impossibly vivid colors matched the trinkets I had received in the first envelope. I scanned the text even as my dad gave me some of the same information.

"It's a school for exceptional people," he said, his words slightly slurring. He reached, grasping for a chair. I grabbed his hand, feeling the strength that was still there, little as it was. Our palms pressed together as I helped him down into it, one-handed. My eyes slid to the additional items as he kept talking. "Only the very privileged go there, Wild, and not privileged in the way of money, but in the way of *talent*. Magical talent."

I stared down at him like a hog looking at a wrist-watch, utterly confused. "Come again?"

He didn't seem to hear me. "I got invited, just like everyone in my family did, but…" His head drooped. "I didn't have what it took. I was a null. A magical nothing…should have had more to me, but didn't."

"A…*magical*…nothing," I repeated. We'd circled back to nonsense words.

"Your mother, though… She was exceptional," he gushed. "So talented. So beautiful, like you, with that long dark hair and amber gold eyes. She was the belle of any ball. And of course, she was the top of her class, just like Thomas. I couldn't go to the academy with her—I didn't pass the trials—but I stayed close to support her. I worked the grounds." He put up his hands. "She didn't talk about it much, but she left because of some family curse. She swore off the magical world and wanted her children to do the same." He shook his head. "And you should've. Thomas should've. I let him go. It was my fault—"

Dad's voice was slurring slightly and I wondered how much moonshine he'd had, but it was clear he believed what he was saying. These fantasy ideas to him were real. At least they were right now when the alcohol was affecting his brain.

"He wanted to go," I said, trying to soak his words up, to hold them close so I could make sense of them. I put a hand on his too-thin shoulder. "He probably would've pushed to get his way. He would've thought it was the right thing to do. All that money, a good education leading to a good job—you couldn't have stopped him. None of us could have, even if we'd known."

Maybe Rory could have, though, I thought whimsically. Tommy had turned to Rory more than once for advice and had always taken it to heart.

Dad sighed and rubbed a hand over the back of his neck. "I suppose you're right." He paused and shook his head. "I thought maybe the neighbor kid and him could watch over each other, like they did growing up."

Confusion smacked me yet again like a two by four to

the back of the head. "Wait, you mean Rory?"

Dad swayed. "We all used to have such a great time, us and Pam Wilson. Pam and your mother were thick as thieves. They were in school together for a while. But then your mother died, and well, that mean ol' codger got heavy into the sauce. He was always bad news. I told her to leave, that I'd help somehow, but what could I do, really? And then there was Emelia in town. She and your mom were good friends too—"

"Dad." I leaned forward and put my hand on his arm, trying to jog him out of the past. I remembered Rory's mom and mine laughing over their glasses of sherry at the kitchen table, but that had been a long time ago when my mother was young and full of life, and my father hadn't been riddled with sickness. "What about Rory? Rory went to that school?"

"That mean old bastard gave me a split lip, do you remember that?" Dad ran his hand over his face. "He was as fast as I ever saw."

Dad meant Buck, Rory's father. Buck had never needed much of a reason to throw a punch. But given that I'd been asking about Buck's son, it meant my dad's grasp on timelines and people were getting confused. I didn't have time to straighten it all out, not that it would've mattered if I had. I'd gotten a couple postcards from Rory from Nevada, the other side of the country from the school

Tommy went to. Besides that, Rory had never lied to me. That was one thing we'd promised each other—we'd always held stock in honesty.

I sat heavily in the chair opposite my dad, my hand sliding from his shoulder. Truth rang in his words, but so did alcohol. There was no telling what was fantasy and what was reality. Not when he was this deep in the moonshine.

"This is the contract, then?" I flipped the pages of the packet, and in a moment, I had my answer. A section at the back laid it all out, right down to the nitty-gritty.

If Billy showed up to the trials, he could keep the money in the welcome packet, and if he was offered a place in the academy, he could apply for financial aid. We were all bound to silence, and our lives would be forfeit if we breathed a word about any of this. Then, at the very bottom, almost like an afterthought, was the line, "If APPLICANT fails to appear at the Culling Trials, APPLICANT stands in breach of contract, and APPLICANT's family will be destroyed."

"It doesn't even make sense," I said softly, reading it again. "At the top it says *if* Billy shows up at the trials. Then at the bottom, it's clear he doesn't have a choice."

I threw the contract down, the papers fanning out.

"They can't make this stick. None of this is legal. They sound like the freaking mafia, not a school for the…privileged." I shook my head. "He's not going. There's no conceivable way they can make him. He's still a minor, for criminy sakes. I'll call the police tomorrow and file a harassment report. I'll turn the money over to them." I flung up my hand, anger eating through me. "If they think we can be bullied into doing what they want, they are sorely mistaken."

My father clasped his hands, staring at the packet with tight, worried eyes. "I tried to call the police after your brother died. I tried to get someone to properly investigate." He swallowed hard. "I should've known better. These people, magical people, have their own laws. Their own set of guidelines. They don't play by the rule book you and I know, Wild, and they don't have to. They have an understanding with certain powerful world leaders. It's been years since I was part of it, but none of that has changed."

There was that word again. *Magical.* Uttered in complete seriousness as though it wasn't straight out of a children's story written by someone with a crazy imagination.

Not something I could focus on at the moment, so I didn't. I ran my hand down my face. "So…what are you saying? What are our options?"

"I don't know. We have to run, maybe. Take the money and try to find someone to hide us."

He was saying that these people—this school for the...talented—would absolutely kill us to get what they wanted. And what they wanted now was Billy.

My little brother with the dimples and the out-of-control hair, the little boy that I'd rocked to sleep more than once when we were little, when Mom was too busy. I wasn't that much older than him, but he...he was mine to protect. Just like Sam was.

I sagged in my seat. I'd never felt so old or so alone, and for the first time in a long while, I desperately wanted my mother. I wanted to lean my head against her shoulder and breathe in the smell of talcum powder and lilacs that was uniquely her. To feel her arms around me and know that she would somehow make it right.

Out of a distant memory, but as if spoken right next to my ear, I heard her say, "*Take the risk no one else is willing to take. You were born for it, my love.*"

My father's voice drifted over the moment. "I thought for sure you'd be next," he said. "I worried I'd have to tie you to your chair to keep you from going. You have less sense than Thomas in that way. But Billy?" He looked up at me, his face stripped of its vitality and the dashing good looks that adorned the pictures on the mantelpiece. "Billy is not even a man yet. And he doesn't have the survival instinct needed for this. Not him."

"I told you, Dad, Billy isn't going." I knew what I had

to do, the plan forming quickly in my mind. I could pull it off. I had years of prep in my own way.

"Wild girl of mine. You follow the wind like you always do," my mother used to say. *"The wind and the wild go together, hand in hand."*

My eyes prickled with a rush of emotion and I dashed any tears before they could fall.

"And tying me to my chair won't work. If they're expecting a boy to fill their ranks—well, then, I need to get a haircut and a sports bra. Instead of Billy, they will get a wolf in sheep's clothing. Let's see how they like that."

CHAPTER 4

I STOOD IN the tiny bathroom of our rundown house, staring at myself in the mirror. The thick, pre-dawn morning air raised goose bumps on my bare arms and across my exposed shoulders. A small tank top hugged my chest over an even tighter sports bra that flattened my already on the small side breasts.

To help Billy, to save him from being forced to go, I'd have to present myself as a boy. Given that he was only sixteen, still fighting his way through puberty, I had a shot.

But I'd have to cut my hair.

I fingered the ends of my thick brown locks, tracing the soft curls that ran to my mid-back. There weren't many things about me that were girly—there weren't many occasions for pretty dresses and makeup in farm life—but my hair was high on that short list. It softened my sharp cheekbones and severe jaw line. It made the tiny cleft in my chin seem feminine and less like Clark Kent's. Without it, my resting bitchface would be boosted to epic proportions, intense enough to make people jump ship in a raging storm to escape me.

I sighed and gingerly picked up the scissors. With this hair, I'd be pegged for a girl, identified as easily as Ronald McDonald in a lineup of hard thugs. It had to go. I had to set the bitchface free.

Heart racing and palms sweaty, I pulled one strand of hair away from my face and opened the blades of the scissors. The first cut was the hardest. After that, it would be easier. It had to, or I'd be sitting here all morning instead of getting on the road, trying to get to upstate New York before my father could pry himself from his chair in the living room and stop me.

"We'll find another way, Wild," he said the night before. "We can take the money and hire someone to hide us. I still have a few connections from my school days—I'm sure one of them will help us."

I'd always thought my father was a terrible liar, the odd one in a family surprisingly great at manipulations and half-truths, although now, I wasn't so sure. While I still didn't know what to make of this magic business, he'd kept information about the academy from us for years. Maybe his fear of the place, or of Mom, had kept him quiet. Because I knew one thing for sure: he was lying through his teeth now.

None of his "connections" would help us. No one

would shelter us from in this particular storm. Someone had to go and pull out the threat by the root, and it most certainly wouldn't be the little boy I'd cared for over the years. He was too pure of heart—too good. He was too much like Tommy.

No, it had to be me. I had the skills to make it, the ability to adapt in pressured situations. I'd tried to remind my dad of all that. *I* was the one who'd brought home Whiskers, the bull that would keep our farm going a little longer. A few years ago, he had been the pride of the livestock auction, anticipated to demand a fat price. But with my fast tongue and an ability to read and manipulate, people, I'd gotten him for a fraction of the cost.

I could use that in this school. I knew I could. And a part of me looked forward to duping the people who'd killed my brother.

But to do all that, I had to cut this danged hair.

"I can do this," I whispered, steeling my courage. I took a deep breath and moved my shaking hand to the dark strand of hair.

"What are you—" Sam's voice went straight through me.

"Ah!" My fingers convulsed and the scissors' sharp edges cut through a chunk of hair.

I sucked in a breath as my sister moved closer. She'd

walked up without me hearing her. The little fart was getting really good at sneaking around.

"Here," Sam said, reaching for the scissors. "I'll help. You need to get going, you're running out of time."

Her lack of surprise was more than telling.

"You listened through the vent, didn't you?" I accused, letting her take the objects of my hair's soon-to-be destruction. She pointed to the small stool and I sat. "Was it just you, or did Billy listen, too?"

"Just me. I remembered that envelope from when Tommy got it. Dad hid it in his normal hiding place that time, and I looked through it. It was the same one, right? With all the money?"

"Yes. This one was meant for Billy." I stared at her in the mirror, seeing the same hard look I wore. Resting bitchface number two coming right up. The women in our family were if nothing else, survivors. I was proud of her for that, proud that she was hard like me. When I left, I knew she'd keep Billy and Dad safe. My heart gave a funny thump I didn't like. I rubbed at my chest, knowing it for what it was.

If I left them, and something bad happened, would they be okay? What if Dad got hurt again? What if the twins got sick? What if, what if, what if. They flowed through my mind, making my anxiety rise with each beat of my heart. They were all I had in this world worth fighting for—but that meant leaving them.

"Billy's too young for college," Sam said.

"I know."

"He's too nice. He believes me half the time when I tell him fibs." Her lips quirked upward.

I smiled back. "I know that too."

"He's too like Tommy." Her voice dipped low along with her brows as she snipped through the strands of my hair. I flinched as if I could feel each cut. "He wouldn't stand a chance at a college—special school or not."

I huffed out a laugh even though I agreed. "He's not as sweet as Tommy—he just seems like it because he uses his charisma and dimples to get what he wants. You'd probably get further if you tried that."

"I have. It's easier just to tell people what they want to hear. It saves time." She shrugged, unbothered by that fact.

I laughed again. Our mother would've been proud of the twins' ability to get out of trouble. I was pretty sure that was a parenting fail. Then again, when you were down on your luck and barely had two pennies to rub together, some careful and harmless manipulation wasn't the worst thing in the world if it got you an improved deal. It was better than taking Robin Hood's approach and flat-out stealing.

"Regardless," I said, worry eating my guts, "you're

right. Billy is not old enough for this. Life has already steamrolled me. He's still too gullible. He'd believe they want the best for him."

"I know," she said softly, slicing through another sheet of my beloved hair.

"It'll be up to you to step in with the ranch. You're better at numbers and managing than Billy is. You've got to make that money last as long as you can."

"I know."

"You can make him cook, though. You're rubbish at that."

Another little smile lifted her lips. "I'm going to be a chef one day, just you watch."

"I believe it." The surest way to get any of us to do something was tell us we weren't capable, to dare us to show our ability. I closed my eyes, no longer able to bear the sight of my shortening locks. "Make sure everyone shares the duties. Don't just take it all on because they are lazy and give you flak. I learned that lesson the hard way with all of you. Don't let them sit in their own stink for too long. You have to yell at Dad sometimes to make him wash up. And he can help in little ways."

"I know."

"And don't lose your head and run off with whatever cute boy you have a crush on this week." I peeked at her in the mirror.

She laughed and shook her head. "Billy wouldn't let me, anyway. He threatens anyone who tries to get close. Not like I need the help."

I chuckled. Yeah, she was going to be more like me than she realized.

"He's protecting you. Tommy and Rory did that with me growing up."

"I don't need protecting. Guys think I'm weak 'cause I'm a girl. But I'll kick them in the balls and take all their money if they mess with me."

I burst out laughing and leaned forward till my forehead touched my knees. Sam swatted me and I sat up straight again.

"I never needed protecting either." The words felt ominous, almost like a jinx. I sure hoped I still didn't need protecting, but I was about to go into the snake pit of the unknown. If my father could be believed and magic did exist, I would be up against a whole lot more than a farmer with a set price for his livestock.

Chapter 5

"PLEASE BE SAFE, Wild," Sam said with tears in her eyes, standing with me at the door.

Light streaked across the sky in layers of yellow, orange, and pink. The sun wasn't far from making an appearance over our struggling farm. A mournful, deep moo sounded in the distance, almost like Bluebell knew I was leaving.

I'll be back, I thought. I wasn't going to end up like Tommy. I would fight as dirty as I had to, so I'd come home when this was done.

I tapped the handle of my knife in its sheath on one hip and then tapped the misshapen crossbody bag hanging over the other hip. The invitation, trinkets, contract, and some of the small fortune were tucked inside. I'd strapped the watch to my wrist.

My father had said that Tommy had gotten close to forty grand, half of which he'd taken with him, just in case.

Turned out my mental calculation had been off. Way

off. They'd given Billy eighty grand.

Eighty thousand dollars!

I'd nearly passed out when we'd counted it and had made Dad count it again to be sure. I couldn't believe so much money was in a wad in a nondescript envelope on the table for anyone to open.

I'd left most of the money behind for the family with instructions on where it would help the most. Ten grand was plenty for me. Having spent my childhood trying to one-up Rory, Mr. Mischievous Bad Boy Lacking Morals, without my brother catching on and taking me to task for acting like a common thief or thug, I was good at getting what I needed when I absolutely had to have it.

"In a game of survival, there are no rules," my mother had always said. *"Play to your God-given strengths, Wild, and don't feel bad for it."*

I would live by that now. Mother said so.

First on the list: steal myself a ride to the airport. A couple days ago I couldn't get the truck to turn over and hadn't circled back to figure out the problem. My bad.

"Take care of everything," I said softly, hugging Sam tightly. "Make up a lie to appease Billy. Let Dad have some moonshine to ease the blow. And stay out of my room. I'm coming back to it."

A tear rolled down her still baby soft cheek. Her red hair flared around her head as the first rays of the sun hit it, a fiery halo. "I guess it's Billy's and my turn to grow up, huh?"

I gave her a sad smile. "That time has come and gone. Now it's time for you to stop being lazy and letting me handle everything."

Her surprised laughter sprayed spit across my face.

"Nice," I said, wiping it away, and with it, my own tears.

"Stay strong," she said, her large blue eyes tracking me as I walked toward the door. I knew she was quoting our mother just as I'd done in my thoughts. "But don't be afraid of your weaknesses. Take every opportunity to laugh. Let yourself cry. I'll hold this place together."

God, how many times had Mom said that? Too many to count. I brushed away more tears and turned away with a nod. I'd let myself cry later. Right now, I had to get going. My time was counting down.

The gravel crunched under my feet as I made my way past the cow paddock and down our long driveaway, thinking of the stranger who'd shown up without a sound.

I still hadn't figured out where the hell he'd gone.

Magic, I heard my father's voice say.

But I swatted the thought away.

Near the junction of the main road and our driveway, I turned right at a packed-dirt path, one I'd taken a million times throughout my youth. But now weeds struggled through the hard crust, trying to reclaim the wildness of the land my two accomplices had pounded flat and clear, running to each other's houses in the long, lazy summer days, or in the wild, storm-thrashed winter evenings.

A strange tingling sensation between my shoulder blades interrupted my thoughts. Rory's parents' house loomed a quarter mile away, a decrepit, sagging structure that should've been condemned years ago. Only his father lived there now. Pam had taken off about when Rory did, leaving Buck with no one to pick on. Leaving him alone with his drinking.

The feeling of being watched coated my body in uncomfortable shivers, my skin twitching like a fly-stung horse. I kept at the same pace, careful not to look around. A predator would attack if they thought their prey had been alerted to their presence.

I nearly lifted my hand to flick my hair, intending to use the movement to covertly glance to the side—only to remember my hair was now cropped close, a shaggy sort of affair that I'd covered up with a dingy old ball cap. Sam had assured me that while the cut would work for a boy, it could be styled into something more feminine if I needed it. I doubted I would need it.

Left devoid of that crutch, I adjusted my bag and

staged a trip, staggering off to the side and looking behind me at the offending clump of nothing. Trees lined both sides of the path and sprinkled the fields beyond, giving someone ample opportunity to hide. Birds chittered a chorus of warning, alerting their fold that a human walked in their midst. The still morning air left leaves and grasses unmolested. No movement caught my notice.

In a measured pace, I kept going, focused on my surroundings, ears strained for any sound.

Because something or someone was there. I was sure of it. Silently stalking me. Mountain lions weren't as common in our part of Texas, but it was a possibility, and they were incredible hunters.

And yet, I knew this was no animal. Humans and animals had always triggered different anticipations and expectations under my skin. Essentially, they read differently when it came to how dangerous they felt. I'd played some intense hide-and-seek with Rory and Tommy when we were kids—to get caught would've meant a pummeling.

Something about the way an animal stalked its prey felt straightforward to me. Scary, but logical. Their motivations were as predictable as their approach. The opposite was true of human hunters. Their style of stalking changed with their mood and emotions, and their ability to stay hidden was enhanced by their increased intelligence.

Humans were the most dangerous predators.

The hairs on my arms twitched, a low level of warning rolling through me that had nothing to do with being eaten, and everything to do with being in far more danger than any animal could bring to the table.

A human, then. An expert with a higher-level intelligence. Apparently, he could move without a sound, hide without disturbing the still foliage, and likely pounce when I was least expecting it.

A pair of dark sideburns and a condensed body of muscle flashed in my mind's eye. I increased my pace. At some point, prey was prey, and it needed to scamper off before the predator took it down. If I was up against the man who'd brought me the envelope, I had no illusions about my role in this game of cat and canary.

I made it to Rory's old house as quickly as I could without looking like I was hurrying.

The same old Chevy sat in the gravel driveway, hardly used anymore by the look of it—cobwebs woven between the mirrors and the body, leaves collecting on the cracked wipers. Buck, Rory's dad, didn't work, preferring to live off of the state, and had no friends to visit. He'd be inside, sleeping off his nightly alcohol binge.

I slipped beyond the brown, scraggly hedge and tiptoed along the side of the house to Rory's old bedroom window. At the base, I paused as a memory from the past assaulted me—Rory clutching my arm, asking Tommy and me not to leave him. I'd been nine at the time, too young to recognize my friend was a scared kid afraid to be alone with the monsters that made up his world. Rory's dad had started shouting then. The shouts had grown louder, accompanied by the soft sound of his mother's sobbing. Tommy was the one who'd known what to do. "Come on," he'd said. "You can stay with us tonight, Rory. They won't miss you."

And they hadn't. Not that night, or the dozens of others he'd spent with us.

That was the first time it had occurred to me that, unlike me, Rory couldn't seek shelter at home. If he did, he'd only find more nightmares. It was why I hadn't batted an eye when he'd said he was leaving this town. And why I would beat the snot out of him if he'd lied to me. You didn't lie to people you shared trust and history with. You just didn't.

I lightly pushed on the window, hearing the soft click that released the broken lock, and flattened my palms so I could slide the window open. A soft squeal made me pause for a moment. An intense itch flared between my shoulder blades.

The stranger was here, watching. I was sure of it.

Sideburns, or one of his minions, was watching me break into this house.

My breath turned shallow, but I didn't stop. He'd basically threatened Billy. I doubted he'd be calling the cops. Besides, we didn't have a working truck and Billy had a deadline—he could do the math.

Trying to ignore the eyes digging into my back, I gritted my teeth against the next squeal and slid the window the rest of the way open. That done, I paused, listening.

A soft rhythmic ticking caught my notice. A clock. Nothing else permeated the thick, gooey silence.

In one swift movement, I pulled myself through the window, stepping onto the strategically placed dresser and the stool beyond it, evidence of Rory's habit of sneaking in and out. In near silence, I tiptoed out of his room, skipping the loose board below the dingy, rust-colored carpet, and paused at the edge of the living room.

No head crested the faded green recliner with the back torn out of it. Leaning to the side, I looked around the chair facing the rabbit-eared TV and spied the couch. Buck's body lay across it, his shoulders as broad as ever and his belly bigger than when I'd last seen him. Crumpled beer cans littered the floor next to an empty vodka bottle on its side.

The expectation of danger slid across my skin as I crossed the threshold into the living room. That was the thing about Buck, he could be blind, passed-out drunk, but if someone messed with his stuff, he could still spring to attention. I'd never understood it. I didn't trust that he'd changed.

I had no choice but to find out.

Silent as the grave, I slipped along the wall to the counter that separated the kitchen from the living area. A badly damaged basket held a pile of junk topped with keys, where they'd always been. Holding my breath, I gingerly lifted them from the mess.

Two keys scraped against each other, a mournful metallic melody. I paused, my heart in my throat.

Rhythmic breathing gently filled the space. Tremors of warning screamed through my gut.

I needed to get out of here.

I eyed the front door beyond the living room. Chances were Buck hadn't kept the hinges greased. That, teamed with his unreal ability to detect when people were messing with his space or his things, meant I would have to head out the way I had come in. Not even Rory had risked taking any of Buck's things out of the front door. That was a dead man's game.

Moving as fast as I could while still being silent, I ducked through Rory's window and slowly closed it behind me. Eyes dug into my back again, almost a physical feeling. I half wanted to turn and sarcastically thank the stranger for waiting. Instead, I jogged toward the truck, time ticking.

It wasn't the watch or deadline that had me moving. It was that miserable sonuvabitch whose property I was still in the process of stealing. He may have lost some of his killer instinct, but I wasn't counting on it. Adrenaline pumping, memories of the fear he'd inspired in my youth battering me, I reached the truck and eased the door open. A loud groan ripped through the silence.

"Crap on a cracker," I muttered as I jumped into the seat and fumbled for the right key. Rookie mistake—I should've plucked out the correct key when I was jogging closer.

I left the door open. The less noise the better. I'd close it when I flung dirt at that bastard's house, not before.

The key clinked as I fit it into the ignition, and I chewed my lip as I turned it. The truck turned over…and over, and over, the engine struggling. When had it last been used? My plan suddenly didn't look so good.

"Come on," I muttered, giving the gas pedal a push before trying again. "C'mon, c'mon…"

The truck cranked to a slow, coughing start.

I heaved a sigh and reached out for the door, chancing a glance at the house as I did so.

The front door stood open.

"Whuddya think yer doin'?" Buck roared as he

stepped around the side of the truck. His huge hand wrapped around the edge of the driver's side door. "Tryin' to steal my truck, you stupid—"

He reached in to grab me with his other massive, scarred hand.

The old coot would beat me bloody without shame.

Terror flooded me, and I reacted without thinking.

I jammed my fingers into that ol' bear's beady little eyes before hammering a fist into his throat. Before he could react, I flung off his reaching hand, and he fell backward with a strangled shout.

I slammed the truck in gear and jammed my foot onto the gas pedal.

The truck coughed and sputtered but caught, slowly rolling forward.

"You filthy, thieving whore," Buck yelled, his voice raspy. He lurched for me again with one eye closed, his reflexes dulled with age and lingering drink. He wasn't giving up though. And neither was I.

I leaned to the side and yanked my arm away. His long fingernails raked across my skin, tearing it open. The truck jerked forward and the door swung shut, catching Buck's body.

He grunted, and I swerved the truck to the right, the quick motion finally wresting his hand from the side of the door. An elbow hit the fender and his body fell away.

I yanked the wheel, swerving the truck in the opposite direction before skidding onto the road. Buck's body rolled in the dust and flying gravel behind me.

"Serves you right," I muttered as I left him behind.

I guess there wouldn't be a question of who stole his truck. Thank God my siblings knew how to work the shotgun. I had less than forty-eight hours at this point—I didn't have time for a nap in a jail cell.

CHAPTER 6

I GRIPPED THE steering wheel of Buck's crappy old truck as I wrestled to keep the entire hunk of junk on the hard curve of the on-ramp. Clearly, it hadn't been left to the spiders just because Buck lacked gas money. The power steering was completely shot.

The brakes squealed like a pair of pigs caught in a noose, and I was pretty sure the signal lights were out, given the level of honking from my lane change. Still, it was better than walking.

With one last crank of the wheel, I was on the highway. "Almost as bad as holding Bluebell," I muttered as I shifted up, the gears grinding.

Foot on the gas, I pushed it to the floorboard in a vain effort to get up to highway speed. The body of the truck shook and rumbled under me, and what was left of the muffler clattered before screeching against cement and falling off—freaking falling off! It tumbled off the road in a shower of sparks that lit up my side mirror.

When I was fairly certain nothing else would fall off,

yet, I rolled the window down and let the fresh morning air blow out the stench of old man and sour beer. A deep breath in and out and my heart rate finally slowed. I was on my way to these Culling Trials, and I had time to spare. Once there, I could convince them that Billy would never be a good fit. That he would be terrible at… whatever they wanted him for.

I lifted my eyes to the rearview mirror and the blood cooled in my veins, sending a shiver right down to my tailbone.

A sleek black sedan, gleaming in the morning sun, pulled into my lane about three cars behind me. The cars between us, annoyed with my lack of speed, passed one by one, but that sedan hung back, allowing others to cut in front.

"Dumber than a box of rocks if they think I don't see them," I murmured, adrenaline racing through me. Nothing that new and shiny would loiter around these parts, happy to go slower than the speed limit. They were here for me.

There was no way I could outrun a slick new sedan, not in Buck's truck.

Fear mingled with the adrenaline and I chewed the inside of my cheek, my mind running through the possibilities. The next exit led into a series of suburbs, schools, and small parks. I could turn off, see if they followed and try to lose them. But if they were aggressive…I'd have no choice but to abandon the truck and lose them on foot.

That would slow me down, and time was not something I'd been allotted a great deal of to get to upstate New York.

I turned my right wrist up to see the face of my new watch. Thirty hours, fifteen minutes, and four seconds left. The flight would take four hours or so, I guessed. The drive to upstate New York maybe another two. I wasn't sure it would work, but I had a crazy idea that might get rid of this tail.

Crazy was my only option at this point.

"I've got time." I cranked the wheel hard to the right and shifted the truck into a lower gear, letting the engine slow the speed rather than the squealing brakes. It clunked along unhappily, but at least it was quieter than the alternative.

I coasted down the off-ramp, wrestling with the steering wheel again as I went around the curve. A glance in the rearview showed me all I needed to know. The sedan had followed me, closing the distance between us, and the sensation of being watched crawled over my skin again.

The difference was this time there was no doubt someone was on my butt.

A part of me was so scared, I couldn't think. Not just

any predator was tracking me, but the ultimate predator, pushing me toward a dangerous future from which I might not escape. Another part of me, however, flared to life, the part that had raced through the fields with Tommy and Rory and broken into abandoned houses. The part that had earned me my nickname.

"I can do this." I shifted down again, and again, until the truck was all but crawling in first gear, the engine grumbling unhappily, chugging and jerking along. I didn't have the vehicle to outrun them. But that didn't mean I couldn't outsmart them.

I rolled the truck to a stop at the bottom of the off-ramp, stuck my arm out the window and waved them by me. Anyone trying to keep their anonymity would surely comply and pick up the tail later.

The black sedan crept forward, closing the distance between our bumpers. It stopped just shy of bumping me, waiting patiently, applying pressure to hurry me along. In the rearview mirror was a stern face wearing aviators and sporting some serious sideburns.

A grin I couldn't control budded on my lips even as warning tingles washed through my body. That man was dangerous. I knew it in every fiber of my being. But he was hounding me, and I didn't take well to that kind of treatment. There were times to back off and times to fight back. My gut told me this was one of the latter.

Here's to hoping that Buck's back-up lights don't work any better than his turn signals.

I shifted into reverse and hit the gas. The engine growled, and the truck shot backward far more efficiently than it moved forward, slamming hard into the hood of the black car. I didn't take my foot off the gas.

"Take that, Sideburns."

The tires of the sedan shrieked on the pavement, but Buck's truck was heavy and made for hauling weight. It shoved the smaller vehicle backward, smoke curling up around it as Sideburns worked the brakes. But I wasn't done yet. Grinning, staring out the back window, I cranked the wheel hard, turning the truck and forcing the sedan into the ditch on the side.

Gravity helped me out and the black car rolled down the steep slope, tires spinning in the dry grass until it bottomed out. There would be no getting out of that without a tow truck.

Still grinning manically, I put the truck into first gear and drove forward. One last glimpse in my rearview mirror showed me a single person standing at the top of the ditch. The sunlight flared off his aviator glasses and those sideburns.

My grin slid away at the look on his face, which those glasses did little to hide.

That lone wolf I'd killed, the one with a taste for cattle, had looked at me like this, with glittering eyes and lips curled over teeth that wanted to tear me apart. I knew without a shadow of a doubt I'd made an enemy that didn't take well to being bested.

As surely as the sky was blue above me, one day, this moment would cost me.

I pressed the gas pedal to the floor and got back on the highway as quickly as I could, fear pricking at me to move faster. To get clear of that wolf's gaze.

The drive was long enough that I had plenty of time to stew, even as I constantly checked my mirrors. I was going to a school where students died and their deaths went uninvestigated. A school for *magically* talented people.

I snorted to myself. If there were real magic in the world, like it was in fantasy books, I would've known about it before now. That was too big of a secret to keep. Maybe my dad had exaggerated, and the school was for kids with exceptional skills in certain areas, more than book smarts.

This time I frowned. As much as I hated it, I could understand why they'd wanted Tommy. He was good at everything he touched. The consummate golden boy who made friends easily and charmed the teachers and got good grades. But Rory had a rap sheet with the local police a mile long for fighting, and his only skills were five-fingered discounts and a knack for shifting the blame to others. None of it made sense.

I sighed to myself as the sign for the airport came up. The answers would come, but I doubted they would just land in my lap. I'd have to hunt for them. At least that was one skill I had under my belt.

I merged into the airport traffic, working to keep the truck from lurching forward into one of the nicer vehicles. Traffic slowed to a stop, caging me in as we approached short term parking.

The engine growled and lurched forward, nearly kissing the shiny red Porsche in front of me.

"Total pig of a truck!" I muttered as I hit the brake hard.

I leaned and craned my head, trying to figure out the hold up. I knew cities were crowded and busy, but with so many people coming and going out of this place, I would've thought they'd have traffic under control.

An SUV inched forward in the right lane, giving me a glimpse of the terminal. My breath caught. Two black sedans glimmered in the morning light. Waiting for someone.

I jerked my head straight and inched forward behind the Porsche. My heart picked up speed, hammering away in my chest so loudly, I couldn't hear the honking around me.

Sideburns apparently had more friends than I did. I watched them from the corner of my eye. Both sedans were new and undented, so neither of them belonged to Sideburns. I swallowed hard, a litany of curses flowing under my breath as I tried to figure out what to do. How did I get out of this pickle?

Buck's truck wasn't exactly what I'd call inconspicuous with its peeling paint, louder than a shotgun blast engine, and the smell of the exhaust rolling out past its non-existent muffler. Then again, I wasn't in the only rust bucket in the airport either. Given that they hadn't climbed into their car or jogged into traffic, I was good for the moment. As long as I kept things calm.

A few more minutes, I checked the time on my watch. Twenty-eight hours, forty minutes, and eighteen seconds to go. Plenty of time.

The numbers shivered as I stared at it, as it went foggy, and then jumbled up like a snow globe being shaken.

"What the hell?" I tapped the screen with one finger. What a junky piece of crap they'd given me…and then the worst thing that could happen did.

The time changed.

And not in my favor.

Six hours left, and counting.

"You piece of donkey crap," I snapped, anger flaring. "Whoever is tinkering with my watch is begging for a shortened life span."

Gritting my teeth, I craned in my seat, seeing a man a few cars up directing traffic into the parking garage. A sidelong glance told me the black sedans were still there.

The minutes ticked by. The truck fought my maneuvering. I kept from looking at the watch, terrified the time would change again.

The airport staff at the mouth of the parking garage waved me to a stop, redundant given the lowered wooden arm next to the ticketing kiosk.

"How long ya gonna be?" he called.

I fought past my heart lodged in my throat. "No time at all. Short. Short time." I grimaced. When had I forgotten how to talk to people? "Just real quick."

"Yup." He waved me on. "Second level. First level's all full up."

I grabbed a ticket, nearly took out the wooden arm as the truck lurched forward too quickly, and parked in a no parking zone on the second floor that was faster than finding a spot big enough to easily fit the badly maneuvering truck. I left the truck running. Maybe someone would steal it. Again.

I bolted for the stairs. I needed to figure out a way past those sedans or I needed to head to the next terminal.

Movement too close behind me fired through my

senses. On pure instinct, I dodged right, putting distance between us. A brick of a man pivoted, not thrown off for long. Another from the other side ran between two parked cars.

The first man lunged for me, nearly grabbing me. I danced away and clipped a car with my hip. The car alarm blared and lights strobed in the dim interior of the garage. My blood pumped through my veins as I spun and landed in a crouch in front of my assailants, two men in suits identical to the one Sideburns wore. They had the same look going on—military short haircuts, aviator sunglasses, and jackets bearing the red Web of Wyrd patch—except these men were both clean-shaven. Apparently, terrible facial hair wasn't standard issue.

The man on the left smiled, but it was cold and reptilian. "Billy. Don't make this harder on yourself."

Billy. They knew who "I" was.

I stayed crouched but scooted backward, feeling my way with one hand. I tried to deepen my voice. "I got a flight to catch, boys."

The two men smiled in tandem and a prickle of a warning snapped me around. A couple of additional men had crowded in behind me and one had what looked like a black canvas sack aimed for my head. I came up with an uppercut that snapped his head back so hard, his sunglasses flew off as he fell backward. My clenched fingers throbbed from the contact. That was going to hurt tomorrow but more for him than me.

I didn't stick around to watch the fallout. I put on a burst of speed as I raced through the parking garage, once more using the cars as leverage, setting off alarms left and right.

I didn't care. Down the stairs and I could see the doors to the airport. I was almost there. Though it wasn't exactly like I'd be home free. They were audacious enough that they'd attacked me in a packed parking garage—why stop?

I dared a glance at the stairwell behind me. Empty.

But that one look back was my undoing. I turned forward to face the main doors as a black bag settled over my head and tightened around my neck.

"Tie him up good. He's a slippery brat."

Hands grabbed at my limbs, pinning me down, and my panic ratcheted into the stratosphere. What the hell was happening? Sideburns had brought the manila envelope that had started this whole mess. Presuming these guys were with him, shouldn't they want me to go to the school?

Suddenly, I was thinking they didn't.

I kicked out, snapping my booted feet free of their hands and driving them into anything I could reach. I connected twice, one blow right after the other. Score one for the girl with long legs.

"He's a big bastard for fifteen!" one of them grunted.

He was an even bigger bastard for a girl, I supposed. Amazons didn't make for easy kidnapping.

I bucked and rolled to the side, getting another shot in on a joint. A knee. Cartilage cracked. Someone swore.

I rolled to the side and broke free, pulling my hands in front of me in time to smack against the hard ground. I was reaching up to rip at the sack off my head when coarse, ridiculously strong hands grabbed me again. These fellers were strong and fast, experienced, and there were too many of them.

I knew when to give quarter to a bigger beast. Just like Whiskers. You had to know when to smack him with a two by four, and when to offer him his favorite treat.

For now, I would give them a mint and let them think they'd won.

Because if I couldn't outfight them, I'd have to outsmart them. I'd have to outwait them.

And then I'd bust their balls when my moment came.

Chapter 7

"I'M DONE," I said, my breath heating up the space inside the bag they'd stuffed my head into. "I won't fight."

"Got some sense in you at least," one of the men growled.

I slumped in their hands, letting them take my weight. The bag over my head stunk like a hippie's armpit and my nostrils flared as I clamped my mouth shut. My wrists were still held out in front of me. I wanted to ask what they were doing but I resisted the urge. I could have fought and yelled, maybe gotten the attention of the other people at the airport, but I had a strong feeling it wouldn't have help. Which meant silence was going to be my friend.

"Hold him tight," one of them said and I tensed as my wrists were squeezed so hard, the tendons rubbed over the bones. With the blood flow to my hands constricted, I barely felt the prick of a blade on my right hand, right in the center of my palm. There was pressure, and then a faint warmth.

I kept my mouth clamped shut, but my eyes caught a glimmer of light from a small hole in the bag. Twisting my head slightly—not enough to alert them but enough to shift the bag—I lined up my left eye with the opening. Through it, I watched as a paper was brought up to my right hand. A contract if I ever saw one.

On impulse, I jerked backward, straining away, but they were ready for me. My body was thrown to the ground. What felt like two guys crouched to either side of me and a knee found the center of my back, pinning me hard. My palms were twisted up painfully, at the edge of breaking, and the brush of parchment paper against my right palm said it all.

I'd signed something, even if I hadn't wanted to.

"Got him. Let's load him up so we can get this run over with."

"No shit, I need a drink and a healer," another guy grumbled.

I was pulled to my feet and my wrists were shoved together as a hard piece of plastic was set around them. Zap straps. Until now, I'd only seen them used on captives in movies.

I strained my wrists apart, to give me space to wiggle if I had to. I was going to be fighting my way out of this as soon as I could, zap straps or not.

The only good thing regarding the bag over my head was it helped me hide the fact that I was a girl. And my sports bra was doing its job seeing as no one had noticed anything in all the wrestling.

I was marched along after that, my feet barely touching the ground, the men around me talking to one another as if I weren't even there.

"Where to next?"

"Arkansas, Missouri, Illinois, Indiana, and Ohio."

"No Kentucky? I thought that was part of our run."

"No."

"Do we need to give Shamus a minute to fix his nose?"

"We're running late. He can do it on the flight. He should've known better than to underestimate one of these kids."

I frowned and sweat beaded up again, sliding down the sides of my cheeks.

One of these kids?

Did that mean I wasn't the only one they were intercepting? What did they want with us?

I pushed the questions from my head. I could ponder them later. The bigger problem was that all those stops would take time. Time I didn't have.

I wasn't going to make my new deadline if I didn't do something.

My mother's voice seemed to float on the air, whispering to me words she'd spoken long ago. I'd been complaining about Rory and Tommy out-fighting me. *"Patience. Wait for the moment to strike. If you hurry the blows, you'll be stuck chasing your prey. You need them to step into your fists."*

At the time, I'd been learning to hunt, but the advice seemed a better fit for this situation. It struck me that a lot of my mother's advice had been…well, let's call it more violent than motherly. Maybe she'd suspected all along that the academy wouldn't leave us alone.

As I was hiked along, a whiff of something tugged at my nose, even through the bag. The new scent was a smell of home, of the farm and something else I couldn't quite put my finger on. A scent of spice and vanilla, easing my fears.

I relaxed, really relaxed, and waited for my moment to come. I had to believe it would show up, and when it did, I would have to be ready to grab it with both hands.

The distant sound of thumping reached my ears, like the rotors of those big helicopters in the war movies Dad and Tommy loved. No, strike that, these *were* helicopter rotors, and I was being led toward them.

If I'd been sweating before, it was nothing to the droplets that slid down my body now. Heights I could do if I kept my concentration on the task at hand, but the idea of being in the air with what equated to a giant food processor above me was not on my bucket list. It was far too easy to imagine being pushed into those blades. Or to remember how easily helicopters crashed in those war movies.

I wasn't sure I could stay relaxed for this part. I slowed my feet, digging my heels into the ground, but I was picked up the minute I put on the brakes, hands on either side of me digging into my biceps and under my armpits.

"Jesus, he's slim but solid," one of my lifters grumbled, and I swung my boot out, catching him in the thigh. He yelped but didn't set me down.

"Knock it off, kid, or we'll throw you out once we're in the air," the man on the other side of me said.

"Yeah, right," I snapped. They would not go to all this trouble just to throw me out. Hopefully.

The spinning rotors were going harder now and the wind that washed off them blew the bag tight to my face. The little hole gave me a quick glimpse of the interior of the helicopter, and the sight made my blood run cold.

A dozen other kids lay on their sides within the flat deck of the enormous helicopter, many in the fetal position. All had their hands tied behind their backs and bags over their heads, just like me. They lay free in the middle of the cleared space, without straps to keep them put or handles to awkwardly grab. As if they might indeed be thrown out for causing trouble.

I did not like this and couldn't think of a way to get out of it.

"Drop him there, next to the girl on the end."

I was boosted into the helicopter and dropped like a bag of grain, left without any restraints like the other kids. The helicopter rotors picked up more speed and then we were moving, lifting into the air. The doors were still open.

This was insane.

"Are you serious?" I yelled as I flattened, the lift of the helicopter making my stomach roll as we rose rapidly.

"You must be from Texas. I can hear it in your accent," the girl next to me said over the din, something that should've been impossible for me to hear without headgear. "You know in Texas, there are places where the number of alligators outnumber the number of people?"

I did a slow turn of my bagged head toward her. Was she serious? We'd been tagged and bagged and left for luggage in a moving helicopter, and she wanted to talk about alligators?

Through my little peephole, I saw her nod as if hearing me. "Death by alligator is a terrible way to go. Not quick at all. First, they pull you under the water, usually clamping down on a hand or foot, which will give you the impression you might be able to escape. Of course, you probably won't. Very few people do, you know."

Good God, how did I get her to shut up? And how was I hearing this over the wash of the rotors?

Magic. The single word whispered through my mind in my dad's voice. No, it couldn't be—

The girl went on, oblivious. "Once they have you under the water, they begin to roll, twisting around and around so they can ideally rip off your limb and bleed you out while at the same time drowning you. Rather effectively called a death roll."

I turned my head away from her, trying to see if there was something within reach I could use to cut through the zap straps. I tried reaching for the knife on my hip, but wasn't flexible enough.

"Then, usually while you're still alive," the girl continued, "they stuff you into their underwater food stash. They prefer their food to be marinated in swamp water and mostly rotted. I think it would make the flesh taste better, to be honest."

"Shut the hell up!" I snapped. "Nobody wants to hear about how alligators eat people!" What in the world was wrong with her?

"I don't want to die!" someone down the line yelled, a guy, I thought, but it was hard to tell with how high pitched his voice was, drunk on panic. "Please. I don't want to die!"

I lowered my head to the floor, pressing my forehead to the only solid thing around, and breathed carefully through my nose. Why had the doors been left open? To scare us? Or did they really intend to throw us out like they'd threatened?

I shivered and found myself thinking about how long it would take to hit the ground, wondering if the bag would come off my head first for one last look at the world. Crap, that girl's death babble had gotten to me after all.

"Death can come in many forms," the girl next to me said, her voice dipping into a monotone that reminded me strangely of Walter Cronkite. "But it is up to us if we embrace it or fight it. I suggest embracing it. We all die. But do we all truly live?"

"Shut up, Wally!" I yelled. "Just shut up!"

"My name isn't Wally—"

"You sound like Walter Cronkite," I said and promptly burst out laughing. Hysterical, hyena-like laughter that ripped out of me. I was in a helicopter with a bag over my head, and the girl next to me was obsessed with death and sounded like flipping Walter Cronkite. This was not real; it couldn't be.

There was only one thing I was sure of. I was going to die.

The laughter cut off as suddenly as if I'd flipped a switch. "I'm not going to die."

"Of course not," Wally said. "And I like that name. I think that will be my nickname from now on. Thank you."

"I don't want to die!" the other fellow yelled again as the helicopter tipped to the side, aiming us toward the open door. I rolled and shimmied, ending up on my ass as I dug my boots into the slick metal for traction. Wally began to slide next to me, the sound of her body scooting across the floor tipping me off.

I stuck my leg out, catching her against my thigh.

"Thanks," she said, as calmly as if I'd offered to hold a door open for her. "Splatting from this great of fall would end my life, I'm quite sure."

Laughter bubbled up again, anxiety-driven and incredulous. Walter Conkrite meets Professor Obvious, this chick couldn't be for real.

"Oh no! Oh no!" the guy from earlier yelled over the sound of a body sliding. "Oh no! Noooo!" His voice reached an octave I hadn't thought possible for a boy of any age before the sound drifted away, along with, apparently, his body. "I'm falling!"

"Oh my God," I whispered. "He fell out. Holy—He really fell out!"

His screams echoed through the space around us,

fading, disappearing, and then weirdly returning, louder and louder. As if he were above us now, still falling. Falling toward us.

"Noooo!" A thud rocked the helicopter, followed by a grunt. "Holy cats!"

It was the guy who'd just fallen out! Was I on drugs? Had they pricked me with a needle when they'd taken my blood?

"Holy cats," he repeated, out of breath. "Am I dead?" The sound of rolling preceded a body knocking into mine. "It doesn't hurt. Oh no, it doesn't hurt. Does this mean I'm dead?" His voice crested to a high soprano. "AM I DEAD?"

Wally laughed. "The dead tell no tales. So you are not dead. It's a miracle, too, given your level of hysteria. I'm surprised your heart didn't stop. You must have a strong ticker. Now, if you'd kept falling and had reached terminal velocity by the time you hit the ground, your bones would have cut through your organs as you would've literally exploded on impact. Messy, but effective in terms of making sure that someone dies. There isn't much that can bring you back from that kind of injury. The body is all but useless at that stage."

"Whu…what?" the guy stammered. "WHAT? WHAT'S HAP—"

There was a thud, and I wiggled my hood to see that

one of the men with the aviators and a black jumpsuit loomed behind him with a billy club.

"What happened?" Wally asked.

"He got knocked out. One of the guards whacked him," I said.

"Too bad. I found his fear fascinating."

I shook my head slowly. "You are seriously weird."

"Of course, I am. So are you. We all are."

"Weird or not, I'm not falling out." I lowered myself to my belly, flattening to the floor as best I could. Behind me, I found a seat leg and I tucked the toes of my boot around it. I didn't know how they'd brought the soprano guy back, but I didn't want to assume they'd do the same for me. I was pretty sure I was on their black list, and maybe letting me fall would be an easy way out.

The sudden pressure on my side said Wally was following my example. "I like you," she said.

"Thanks?"

"I'm going to stick close to you, I think. I have a good feeling that you'll be strong."

I grimaced. "Lucky me." But the strange thing was, something about Wally was calming. Her knowledge of how people could die was nothing short of morbid, and yet the more she talked, the less it bothered me. I didn't mind. Not really. Maybe she wasn't so bad. At least her babbling helped distract me as we landed and picked up someone else, also in a black hood from what I could see through my peephole. Unlike me, though, the other kids weren't fighting the men. Why not? What did they know that I didn't?

Time. Which I had to be nearly out of, although I had no way to check with my hands zap strapped behind me.

Through Wally's ongoing chatter, one thought kept cycling through my head—an apology to Dad. To Sam and Billy. *I'm so sorry. I screwed this up. I'm so sorry.*

We stopped five times in total after my pick up. I rolled the states through my mind. Arkansas, Missouri, Illinois, Indiana, and Ohio. We were getting closer to New York at least, but how close? Could I find a way out of this mess?

After the third stop, I stopped thinking about anything but getting the zap straps off and having a pee. My wrists were numb, but my bladder surely was not and each bump and drop of the helicopter made the urge worse.

"I think we're almost there," Wally said, breaking off her monologue about paper cuts getting infected and going gangrene in a rather small number of people—a freak occurrence, but an unfortunate way to go. Hardly heroic.

"Almost where?"

"You don't know?" She sounded genuinely surprised.

"I mean, you *really* don't know?"

The helicopter began to descend rapidly, throwing us all into the air for a split second, the lack of gravity making my belly roll. As we dropped and hit the floor once more, my heart rate skyrocketed. There was no time to ask Wally what she meant, and really, I didn't need to. I'd been a fool not to figure it out earlier. Anyone who threatened a family would do something this insane and violent.

They'd given me a ride. How sweet of them to wrap me up like a present.

And now, we'd arrived at the Culling Trials.

CHAPTER 8

A POPPING SOUND filled the interior of the helicopter as if a balloon had been burst, and the steady drum of rotor blades assaulted my senses. Something had definitely been hampering the sound so we could all hear one another speaking without headsets. Now, there was nothing but noise and darkness, mitigated only by that one tiny peephole that had become my salvation for the ride.

Something hard brushed against my back. A knee. The bag was ripped off my head, and light bit into my eyeballs, as jolting as the onslaught of sound. I ducked my head and squinted as my wrists were tugged. My hands came free, tingling and numb as strong fingers curled around my upper arm.

"Time to show us what you're made of." I heard the words still audible over the helicopter as though they'd been delivered right to my ear. The familiar voice sent shivers down my spine.

I blinked my eyes opened, forcing myself to acclimate

to the sound and light. Shorter than me still and built stockier with a hand that seemed made out of pure metal was my old friend.

Sideburns.

"What are you doing here?" I asked, sounding as lame as someone could. It was all I could think to say. This was obviously his gig, and my rough handling was likely by his instruction.

Sideburns jerked me past the bodies of other kids in the helicopter, my feet catching on limbs and my weight tipping forward. Shouts and yelps were reduced to muffled cries by the helicopter's noise. He held me up and all but dragged me to the edge, my feet edging out into space as we started to land.

My jaw dropped. Five other large army helicopters had landed ahead of us, with three more still in the air waiting to touch down. Before us loomed an enormous twenty-foot-high stone wall covered in ivy. The wall stretched in both directions, broken only by thick metal gates, five in all, that looked like they'd been there a very long time. Sentries lurked atop each gate, looking down on the strip of land before them, their bodies poised and hands holding guns or nothing at all. They each looked to be assigned to certain portions of the ivy wall.

More shivers attacked me. For some reason, those sentries without weapons made me the most nervous.

Kids tumbled out of helicopters that had already landed, falling into the dirt and scrambling to get up and wipe their eyes or rub their wrists. Others stood in lines or clustered in groups, occasionally shoved this way or that by handsy men or women dressed like Sideburns.

All of that paled with the realization that the sun had hardly moved from when I'd been grabbed at the airport. I felt like I'd spent a whole day traveling, but the position of the sun said it must've been no more than a couple hours.

Magic.

I didn't get a chance to dwell. In the distance, rising above the cacophony of sound, roared an enormous beast.

"What is this place?" I asked quietly as the helicopter bumped down.

"Your future. Or your grave," Sideburns said, somehow hearing me. He jerked me to the right. "The choice is yours."

"Clearly it isn't, since you kidnapped me and brought me here." I resisted him slightly, just to make him work for it. What could he do, kidnap me again?

"The most important lesson one of your kind needs to learn is how to adapt." He directed me off the helicopter and toward a table surrounded by wide-eyed kids who all blinked in a daze.

"One of my *kind*?"

He shoved a girl with straight blonde hair to the side before grabbing the shirt of a tall lanky kid and ripping him the other way, making a path for us. The kids from my helicopter were just now tumbling from its belly, landing on the dusty ground. Apparently, Sideburns holding a grudge meant I got preferential treatment. Yay me.

"Time to wizen up, or you'll get dead faster than you can cry for your mama," he growled.

"Ah." I nodded as he pushed me against the table. "You have superior linguistics. Quite the professor."

He reached around to a large pocket on his side and pulled out a hat—my hat! I didn't even remember losing it. He slapped it onto my head and pulled it down taut. A cold feeling washed through me, wondering if he knew exactly who I was. How couldn't he? But if he did, why would he be playing along?

"Johnson, Billy," Sideburns barked at the table attendant, an equally hard-faced woman with a jaw that could chop boards.

She glanced at me then down at her computer, her fingers tapping the keys with a staccato that blurred her surprisingly bright red nails. The kids around us pushed away, their tight-eyed gazes flicking to Sideburns and then quickly away. He clearly made people nervous.

"He's young for the trials. Have you got the appropriate permissions?" she said without inflection.

No kidding, "Billy" was too young. All of the kids crowding into the strip between the helicopters and the imposing walls looked like recent high school graduates. My age. The same age Tommy had been when he'd left. I didn't know what was in store for us, but it was clear that it was dangerous, and my younger brother wouldn't have stood a chance.

"That has been cleared, all permissions granted," he replied, lying with ease.

"What do you have against my family?" I asked without meaning to.

The woman's eyes flicked up as a handheld machine resting on the table beside her computer bleeped blue lights. She pointedly looked down at her computer.

"Not me," Sideburns said in a low voice, for my ears alone. "But our world? That's a whole other issue with you and your family."

I didn't have time to process that statement. The woman ripped off a piece of paper that had emerged from the machine and handed it across the table. A name tag with Billy's name and the word "Shade" under it.

Sideburns snatched it up before grabbing the wrist with the watch and pulling it out over the table for the woman, forcing me to bend over or lose an arm. He peeled the backing off before slapping it onto my chest, his hand briefly covering my breast before pulling away.

I froze for one heart-stopping moment, staring at myself in his aviators, knowing that he was looking at me from behind them. A tense beat passed in which I wondered if he'd felt my flattened boob. I was skinny by boy standards even though I was all lean muscle—no way could that little squishy area pass as a pec. The sports bra had it smooshed tightly to my chest, but it was still a breast, and they felt different than anything on a man's body. A guy like Sideburns would know that. Despite the bad choice of facial hair and the hard lines etched into his face from constant scowling, he was a looker. He would know his way around a female's anatomy, or a man's, if that was his thing.

The thought rose up again: If he knew who I really was, why was he playing along?

Uncertainty churned my gut.

The beat lengthened as a machine beeped in the background. My watch vibrated against my wrist. In the distance, three helicopters lifted into the air, leaving their human cargo behind.

"All set," the woman said.

Sideburns turned, and my exhale gushed out of me. If he knew—and how could he not—he didn't plan to reveal me. He grabbed me by the arm again and yanked, taking me back in the direction of the helicopter that had dropped me off, its interior empty now. It shuddered before lifting into the air.

"Watch yourself," Sideburns said, pulling me past a gate where a group of kids with name tags waited, shifting and fidgeting with nervousness or maybe anticipation. A few of them were grinning, which seemed out of place after a ride like that. What the hell was going on?

He walked me toward the last gate, and as we neared it, I saw that the ivy covering the wall wasn't the lovely docile plant I'd originally thought. Inch-long barbs covered the vines, and the leaves had fully serrated edges, scratching in warning against the concrete wall. Like nails on a chalkboard, the sound made my teeth clench.

Sideburns finally stopped, but he didn't back away. "Your strength has always been in adapting. This is no different. Adapt and follow your gut instincts. Don't question your intuition, and don't shy away from your nature. Do whatever it takes to stay alive. Always. That is your only chance."

I stared at him, mute, as he let go of my arm. Kids shied away from us, their widening eyes following him like they were sheep staring at a wolf in their midst. His advice made it sound like he knew me. Like he was a coach who needed to remind his star player of her training before a big match.

Her, because he surely knew, I realized that now. He knew and he let me stay anyway. Why?

Strangely, his words hit a primal place deep inside me. I felt their rightness. Their poignancy. Something within me responded to his suggestion.

"Stay strong," he said before glancing at the huge iron gate in front of us. "And stay here. This will be the easiest course for you to get through while your mind is spinning."

He nodded, as though I'd agreed, before striding away, his shoulders straight and head high, parting the anxious students.

"What just happened?" I muttered to myself.

I barely noticed the slight girl with large brown eyes and heavy black lashes drift in beside me, her gaze fixated on Sideburns.

In her strangely deep voice, the one that reminded me of Walter Cronkite and his nightly news specials, Wally said, "Life is eternal, when you know the right people."

Movement at the top of the wall caught my attention as more kids filed in around me. A huge wolf prowled near the edge, looking down at the kids gathered in front of the gate. It passed in front of a stoic individual with a large knife attached to a belt around her black clad hips. A sword scabbard jutted out behind her on the other side, the weapon attached to her back within easy reach. The wolf didn't react to her presence. She didn't appear to notice it stalking along.

"What is happening?" I breathed, my heart ratcheting up. Wolves did not ignore humans like that.

"Hello." The slight girl stepped in front of me and stuck out her hand. Her head barely reached my chin. "I'm Drexia," she said in a squeaky voice, drastically different from the deeper one she adopted when delivering odd statistics that had little relevance. "I'm named after my beloved Nana, God rest her soul. My friends call me Wally."

I couldn't help a smile. "I'm the one that called you Wally, actually. In the helicopter."

"Yes," she said.

Okay. I guess that meant we were friends now.

I lifted my eyebrows, not really sure where to go from there. To say she was an odd duck would be a bit of an understatement.

The last of the helicopters lifted from the ground, showing the natural land behind them, covered in dense foliage and gently rolling hills. The helicopters hadn't been for show—I could feel it. There wouldn't be civilization for miles. We were at the mercy of whoever ran this show.

"What's your name?" Wally asked, holding her hand out to me.

"Wild." I grimaced, quickly deepening my voice to cover my mistake. "Billy, actually. It's Billy."

"Wild. I like that better. Hi, Wild." She didn't lower her hand.

"Hey." I took her hand in a sure grip, not having to pretend to have a strong handshake. Running a farm, you dealt with men a lot, and a handshake said a lot about a person. I had learned quickly to make it firm. No limp handshakes were allowed in Texas.

The deep roar I'd heard earlier shook the ground and clattered my teeth, still way in the distance but no less potent. The wolf from before passed along the wall in the opposite direction, and though I couldn't see for sure, it felt like its eyes were beating down into me.

"The Tyrannosaurus Rex, often referred to as the T-Rex, lived around sixty-eight to sixty-six million years ago in what is now western North America," Wally said as she stepped in beside me.

A red-headed kid I immediately named Freckles pushed his way to my other side. "Why'd the Sandman bring you over here?" Freckles asked over Wally droning on about T-Rexes and their eating habits.

"The Sandman?" I asked, watching that wolf make its way past us yet again. "How is… Why… Am I seeing things?"

"To date, in this century, there has never been a death

by mauling as it pertains to the T-Rex," Wally said within the ebb and flow of nervous chatter around us.

"Yeah, the Sandman," Freckles said, apparently not realizing that someone else was also talking to me. It was a miracle I could focus on anything outside of a massive predator walking the walls of some sort of death compound. "He has the most career kills of anyone of his kind. Rumor is he's a millionaire from all the high-dollar contracts he's taken, but he doesn't do too many anymore because he's bored. He needs a bigger challenge. That's why he became a teacher in the House of Shade. Rumor is he's creating his own army. This is his first year of recruiting. Did he say anything to you?"

"To date," Wally said, fingering a button on her sweater as she watched the top of the wall, "in this century, the Sandman has laid to rest over one thousand people that we know of, the most lethal in the House of Shade, driving fear into the hearts of the students, and creating discourse between the faculty and the school headmaster."

"Yeah. Him," Freckles said. "Do you know him?"

"He threatened my family if I didn't show up." I glanced down the wall before pushing up onto my tiptoes. Six feet might not have set any records for height, even for a girl, but it was usually tall enough to see over a crowd of people.

More groups of people waited down the way, each clustered in front of one of the gates. A few people stood closer to the wall, but most were pushed back in a big horde, shifting and fidgeting in a way that indicated they weren't excited about what lay beyond. It spoke of the unknown. Of nasty surprises.

"Oh." Freckles nodded like my answer made all sorts of sense. "You must've been on the 'hard case' roster and gotten unlucky with him. A lot of people didn't think he'd do well as a recruiter for the House of Shade because he's lacking in his manipulation techniques. Clearly he found another way that suited him better."

I frowned as I looked down on Freckles, seeing the logic in what he was saying, but bewildered all the same by the lingo. "Huh?" was about all I could muster.

"Yeah, he probably brought you up personally to prove a point. Man, that sucks." Freckles shook his head and shifted to the side. A lithe and beautiful woman walked along the edge of the wall, a serene smile on her face and a stick in her hand. "This place is scary enough. I can't imagine dealing with his threats on top of it."

"The House of Wonder." Wally's voice dropped. "Beware that which beguiles and delights, for a blade is hidden under the mage's robe."

"What is this place?" I asked as the beautiful woman passed in front of the black-clad woman, who was so still,

I almost lost track of her presence. Almost.

Wally turned her gaze to my face. "Did your parents not tell you of this place? I wondered about that in the helicopter, a metal beast not meant to fly."

I shook my head. "No, they must have forgotten to include it in their bedtime stories."

"They didn't tell you anything?" Freckles asked, turning to survey me as well. "Why not?" He tilted his head in commiseration. "Did they think it was cheating? Yeah, my dad said I should experience it blind, like he did. That it would make a man out of me. But my mom walked me through everything I might face. Don't worry, I'll help you, man."

"Attention, everyone." The speaker was the beautiful woman who'd walked past us, and although I could barely see her now, her voice rang out with perfect clarity. "Attention, please."

The noise and chatter from the ground died down. A few fingers came up to point.

The woman continued to make her way along the wall until she stood in what I assumed was the center above the middle iron gate.

"Welcome to the annual Culling Trials." She lifted her hands to the sky and a cheer rose from around me and on down the way from all the other kids. "Here is where we will test your mettle. Your strength. Your speed. Your know-how. Here is where you will learn if you have what it takes to advance into the Academy of Shadowspell, or if you'll be doomed to a life…of *lesser.*"

A wave of chatter followed her pronouncement. Feet shifted and scraped against the dirt. Bodies pressed in tighter, the anxiety and excitement palpable.

"I really hope I make it through," Freckles said softly. "My dad said he would disown me if I didn't. I mean, he was joking, but…" Freckles's voice reduced down to a soft mutter. "I'm pretty sure he was joking…"

"Eight out of ten make it through the first stage of the Culling Trials," Wally said, still worrying that top button of her sweater as she watched the woman on the wall. "Nulls and those not physically capable often drop away, leaving able-bodied magical types to advance to the academy, a cutthroat smorgasbord of treachery and betrayal. The academy is what squeezes you. Bends you. Finally, breaks you. One in eleven of those who leave the trials ring the bell and excuse themselves, hanging their heads in shame. The rest are forced to leave, unfit and destitute, for a half-life with the Norms. Forever known as dropouts and failures. Lesser."

"Wow. She's a real downer," Freckles murmured. "Who can even do all that math?"

Wally's voice dropped. "You do not choose the academy. The academy chooses you."

"What the hell?" Freckles leaned around me to get a better look at Wally.

As Sideburns—the Sandman was too cool of a name for that guy—had predicted, my mind spun. A magical academy? Assassins? Wall-walking super wolves? Even though my dad had told me about some of it, I hadn't believed him.

But seeing what was in front of me now...how could I not?

I wasn't up for any of this. Hell, I *was* an ordinary person. I'd always been.

My mother's voice rose up out of nowhere, taking over my thoughts.

"There is magic all around us, Wild. Everywhere. In everything. In you. You gather people to you like moths to a flame. You were built to ride the wind, my love. So ride it. Your time will come."

Very little of that had made sense at the time. I'd been in the middle of getting in trouble for convincing my brother and Rory to follow me into the neighbor's bullpen, sure we could tame the mean old bugger with the single horn and a seriously bad attitude. I'd nearly gotten us killed. Dad had been too livid to deal with me, so he'd passed me off to my mother to finish the tongue lashing and decide on a punishment.

She'd decided on no punishment. Tommy had fumed

and even Rory had been disappointed, both wanting me to get my butt whooped for convincing them to take the risk. Instead, no one had been blamed, not even them for going along with it.

When mom had said all that about magic, I'd never, in my wildest dreams, thought she was talking about real magic, the kind in children's books. Yet here I stood with a bunch of people who'd apparently been raised on this stuff along with their Wheaties.

"Say goodbye to your contact with the outside world," the woman continued, her hair dramatically blowing behind her as if she were a model across from a fan, and even though I couldn't see it from the distance, I knew she had a sweet smile on her face. A fake smile that hid a gleaming blade, like Wally had said. "Cell phones are useless. There will be no computers, no social media, no GPS. There will only be your courage and your mettle. Your watch will help us monitor your progress through each trial. If you take it off, your time here will be forfeit. Make it to the end for full points. Grab the gold for a bonus. And, as always, keep your friends close, and your enemies closer. I will see you on the other side."

She sauntered off to the side and held her stick high. With a flick of the wrist, the heavy metal gates that stretched out down the wall clunked before us, shuddering. They opened, little by little. The creaking sound of metal riding the roar of what Wally seemed to think was a freaking T-Rex. People pushed in behind me, but no one attempted to get ahead. A quick look down the line showed the same thing at each gate. Groups of people, no one stepping forward.

That faint smell I'd caught earlier rode the moment. Dirt and sweat and spicy vanilla. A smell of home and comfort. Of kicking ass and causing mayhem.

A slow grin slid over my lips and I clung to the words of my mother.

"You were born to ride the wind, Wild."

Chapter 9

"What's the strategy?" I grabbed Wally on one side, Freckles on the other, and stepped toward the gate in front of us. I'd be damned if I was doing this alone, and they seemed to know what to expect. We'd be stronger together, something I'd learned from my childhood with Tommy and Rory.

"Okay." Freckles hurried beside me, jogging to keep up with my longer legs. "The person on top of this section obviously belongs to the House of Shade, which is what this stretch will be dedicated to. If the Sandman was your recruiter, then you're probably in your element."

"You said they kill people. You think that's my specialty?" I asked incredulously.

"Creating walking memory banks, that's mine," Wally said.

"Oh gross, you're not a necromancer, are you?" Freckles groaned at Wally. "That's the type of thing one of them would say. Dead people shouldn't be used for information recall. It isn't right. It just isn't."

"There is comfort in rising from the dead," Wally replied as the gate in front of us opened wider. We were nearly there, leading the pack of not-so-eager participants.

"No, that's *not* comfortable," Freckles said as a warning blared through my mind and ran all the way down my spine. "Coming back as a rotting corpse after dying is *not at all comfortable!*"

"Wait," I said, slowing as we reached the now-open gate. I grabbed Wally and stepped to the side. Freckles fell in behind us.

"What's the matter?" Wally whispered.

A narrow path led from the gate into a forest of dense redwood trees. Green grass filled in between artfully tangled weeds and the occasional shrub that would easily tangle a foot should someone go running through them.

The pack of kids behind us slowed, and I knew without knowing how that everyone was waiting for someone else to go first. Why wouldn't they? We were walking into a house of freaking predators who were known for killing people. Even if this was some elaborate joke that I would not find funny, Sideburns was part of it, and his sense of humor was obviously dangerous. Boogeymen lurked in this place, and they had the upper hand.

I took Wally's wrist for the same reasons I would've taken Tommy's back in the day—half for comfort, half to get the show on the road. A sudden pang of loss hit me. Had he paused at this gate like I was doing? Had he waited for someone to grab his wrist like I'd always done in potentially dangerous situations?

"Go through or go around?" I asked quietly, walking forward slowly. This wasn't unlike walking through the wilds after an animal had gotten onto our lands and killed livestock. I needed the same awareness. The readiness to act.

"My mom said that most people went around, but she'd wished she'd gone through," Freckles said. "But she never talked to anyone from this house."

"In the academy's history, three percent of those who have gone through the middle have died," Wally whispered. "Sixty-five percent made it to the end."

"How many people died the other way?" Freckles asked.

"None," she replied as a group of tough-looking boys broke from the pack. They went right, avoiding the path, at a slow walk. "But only fifty percent of them made it through."

"So we have a better chance of making it through if we go through the middle, but we might die?" Freckles's voice increased in pitch. "What kind of odds are those?"

"Better odds than hang-gliding in a hurricane," Wally replied, cool as a cucumber.

"Why are you so good at math and so stinking bad at social skills?" he screeched, bringing his voice up a few octaves, and I was suddenly pretty sure he was the screecher from the helicopter. "It's not natural."

A group of five girls dressed all in black, down to the painted fingernails they held near their chests, walked around us toward the path, giggling as they did so. Outwardly they looked nervous and silly. They looked like they'd get taken down, no problem. But the fluidity in their gait and the seriousness in their eyes told a different story.

A story I had no trouble reading.

If I'd seen this group slip into the park in town at night in my hometown, I would have instantly known they were up to no good, that this wasn't their first rodeo, and any attempt to follow them, even out of curiosity, would lead to retaliation.

Something within me clicked into place. A strange understanding.

"They belong here," I said, marveling. "Wally, of the sixty-five percent who make it through, how many end up in this house?"

"Yes. Good question." She paused. "Eighty percent of the sixty-five percent, I believe. A larger percentage of the ones who make it through the other way are not native to this house."

"It's unnatural what she's doing," Freckles repeated. "It is literally another language, and only the criminally insane speak it."

A short guy with a stick, much like the woman on the wall had used, strutted forward, leading the way. Dumb as a post, I could tell. He grinned for the people behind him, his audience, and gave a mocking half bow before stepping onto the path.

I knew what he was thinking: If a bunch of silly girls can do this, obviously I can.

A grin crept up my face.

Those girls were luring the over-confident morons after them. They felt confident in these surroundings, and their intent was to do harm to those that didn't understand what they were up against.

"Fascinating," I said, my heart quickening even as my stomach pinched. "I mean, super messed up, but…wow."

The Bro glanced at his watch, gave his fan club a grin, and walked forward. Immediately, a small crowd hurried to follow, the guys all bravado and the girls twittering and laughing nervously.

Hook, line, and sinker, the dumb fish were caught.

"Let's go," I said, grabbing the two by my side and hurrying after the Bro Pack.

"Okay, that was a lot of math back there, but isn't this the bad way for people like us?" Freckles said, trotting beside me, his round face already sweating.

"For us, yes," Wally said, not needing my tug to stay with me. "For him?" She nodded to me. "We shall see."

Releasing their arms, I said, "It's a bad way for all of us, yes," forcing myself to slow as we neared the path. I needed to think this through.

Logic said to go around. Hell, statistics said go around. No one had died the other way. Sideburns might've thought I'd do well in the House of Shade, and someone obviously thought this was my—strike that, Billy's—place, but I didn't know about that. I didn't know about any of this. We should take the easier approach, the one favored by those who didn't belong in the house.

Except…

Something about the girls' approach pulled at me. Dragged me behind them. And it wasn't just a sick fascination, or the weird heaviness in the pit of my stomach that said their actions fit with the danger of this place. They were taking others along this path for a purpose. In this game of survival, they'd thought it necessary to bring bait. They knew what they were doing. It made sense to tag along and ride their coattails, so long as the Bro Pack stayed between us.

Don't shy away from your nature. Do whatever it takes to stay alive. Always.

"Okay, Sideburns," I said under my breath, stopping

just before the path. "You win."

I stepped onto the center path with one foot, then the other. My watch vibrated and a message flashed across the screen.

You've chosen. Good luck.

Something bumped my back, pushing me forward, but a quick backward glance showed me nothing was there.

I spun, wide-eyed, and put out a hand. My palm found a hard nothingness separating me from the path, or lack of a path, I hadn't taken. Like plexiglass, only it wasn't glass and it wasn't visible.

Wally and Freckles stood side by side, staring at me on the other side of the invisible barrier while the Bro Pack's loud talking and laughing echoed as though we were locked in the same ethereal chamber.

My chest constricted and I struggled to breathe.

Magic. Real, honest-to-God magic had trapped me on this path. The small hold-out part of me that still hadn't believed could no longer deny the truth. "What's your name?" I called to Freckles, not sure why that should be so important right then but needing to know. Maybe just in case we all ended up dead.

His brow creased and he leaned forward a little. His lips soundlessly formed the word *what?*

"What's your name?" I said again, knowing I needed

to turn and hurry to catch up with the Bro Pack, but feeling the urgency here, as well.

He frowned and shook his head a little before stepping forward.

"What?" he asked, placing his second foot, his voice now loud and clear.

I sucked in a breath, guilt tearing through me as I looked down at his feet, both firmly on the path. His watch vibrated. After he'd read it, his eyes hit mine.

I'd just accidentally lured him in. I'd learned from those girls and immediately applied the lesson without intending to.

"What's your name?" I asked softly, an apology under my words, cursing the Sandman for dragging me into this. Cursing my parents for never explaining what I might someday be forced into.

"Oh. Pete. Just don't call me Peter. My brothers always tease me about Peter. I mean, it's a person's name, not just a dick's name." He rolled his eyes—"Anyway"—and put out a fist.

Handshakes I had. Fist bumps weren't part of the old farmer language. They made me feel awkward for reasons unknown.

"I'm…Billy." I caught myself just in time. "Sorry, Pete, if you didn't want to come this way," I said, feeling like it was my duty to clear the air. Then, remembering that the guys I knew didn't usually apologize—they were more apt to find someone else to blame—I amended, "But you did step through, so…your bad."

Wally pushed up behind us, shoving Pete out of the way. "I couldn't hear you guys. What'd I miss?"

"That's Pete." I hooked a thumb at him.

"Hello, Peter," Wally said professionally, putting out her hand for a handshake, same as she'd done for me.

Pete scowled at her. He hurried after me. "Of course, I was going to come. The Sandman ushered you over here. He only pays attention to the best. My best shot of getting through is to hang with you, man."

I laughed sardonically. They couldn't possibly know that my brother was the one Sideburns had attempted to lure here and got me in his place. I didn't understand his game, but he hadn't denied my family was a target and he hadn't cared that I'd shown up instead of Billy. Good thing I knew something Tommy didn't.

I knew how to fight dirty.

Chapter 10

The Bro Pack meandered along ahead of us, through the tall trees, reaching out and touching them here and there. I resisted the urge to do the same. Whatever this place was, I wasn't trusting it and that meant no touching if I didn't have to. The two girls at the back hung onto each other, looking to either side fearfully. They were way out of their element in this trial if their balayage hair and designer clothes were any indication. Both of those things were great for us. Whatever beasties lurked in this place would pick off the weakest prey first. Which was most certainly them.

"We're going to use them as chasers," I said, keeping my voice just low enough for Wally and Pete.

"What?" He frowned up at me, brow crinkling.

"A chaser," I repeated, somewhat surprised that he didn't know. "A car ahead of you on the road that's speeding. You tail them, and if a cop is waiting in a speed trap, they'll get the chaser car first. What kind of dude doesn't know that? It's like Driving 101."

He flushed and I almost felt bad. "I don't have my license yet," he mumbled. "But I played Gran Turismo a lot."

That had to be a video game, something I'd never played. Growing up, I'd considered myself lucky if I got a turn to pick what was on TV a couple times a week.

I held up both hands, feeling the need to get moving. "Let's push in close to them. We need to follow closely enough to see what comes at them, but not so close that we get caught up in it. Got it?"

I started forward and they fell in beside me. Wally clasped her hands in front of her.

"Two miles of No Man's Land is the typical length of each of the trials," she said. "Though those that run them often claim they're far longer."

"I can't run one mile, never mind two!" Pete's face bloomed a bright pink as if he were already running.

I spared him a glance. "If we do this right, we won't be running."

We'd taken no more than a few steps when the light around us dimmed to an unnatural twilight. Deep shadows pooled between the trunks of the trees and hid the path ahead.

Then the entire scene shifted right in front of us.

"Holy cats," Pete whispered.

That wasn't the word that went through my mind.

The trees shifted and spun, dizzying me. Then they grew, their limbs shooting up and out, changing color and appearance as they did until we were surrounded by towering buildings. The ground below us hardened rapidly, turning from dirt to concrete. In the distance, the sound of traffic cut through the night instead of the birds and soft rusting of leaves.

"We're in a city," Pete said.

"Nothing gets past you," I muttered.

Dead ahead was an alley that cut between a series of buildings. At what had to be the end, I could see a sign blinking in the distance, well above our heads. Exit.

"Here we go," I said. The anticipation of our first challenge intensified in me until I was wound tighter than a dollar-store guitar.

Wally crowded in on my one side and tried to slip an arm through mine. I shook her off.

I needed my hands free for what was coming.

"Can you see those idiots that were ahead of us?" I asked.

"No," they chimed in unison.

Well, that settled that. "Sorry, Pete, I lied," I said as I broke into a jog, heading deeper into the alley.

Pete groaned. "I knew I should have cut out the Snickers bars. I should have gone to the gym."

"Every year, thirty-five to fifty-six people die from

ingesting peanut-laden chocolate bars, not realizing they are allergic to the peanuts. Even more people die from cardiac arrest while attempting to get into shape. Fifty-year-olds drop dead from running on a non-regular basis. You should be grateful—you dodged two deaths."

"Except now I'm running," he wheezed.

"Yes. Your odds of making it through this are dropping dramatically," Wally said solemnly. "Good luck."

My lips twitched. I wasn't even sure she knew she was being funny, which only made her funnier.

The alley was easy going, smooth with no visible obstacles—and *that* made me nervous. There was a sudden shout up ahead, then a series of shouts that turned into screams. A normal person would have stopped, maybe turned and made a run for it.

I picked up speed, following instincts hammered into me my whole life. If someone screamed, you hurried to help.

Pete and Wally hissed at me to slow down, to stay back, to take it easy, but I kept running until the alley came to a T-intersection. I paused there, waiting for a noise to pull me in one direction or the other.

A whimper, barely above a whisper, drew me to the left. I crouched, pressing my hip against the building as my hand slid to the knife sheath on my other hip. I pulled the homemade blade free.

Just in case.

A small part of my brain tried to point out the insanity of what was happening, which didn't follow any pattern I'd learned over the last eighteen years of life. The voice was only trying to keep me safe, but I'd gotten good at telling it to shut up.

A light above a doorway on the other side of the alley flickered to life. At the base of the entrance lay a crumpled figure, blood clearly visible against his hair. I'd seen him with the Bro Pack at the beginning. The smallest of the bunch, he was fair-haired to the point of being white blond and slight, barely five feet, if that. Sam would have outweighed him, and she was a waif.

The shuffle of boots on the pavement.

"Don't leave me," the crouched figure whimpered, curling tighter around himself.

"Kill the goblin, we don't need him," a voice shouted from the other side of the light. Highbrow, cultured, and cruel, the voice was the epitome of good breeding gone terribly wrong. My lips curled. And then my brain tried to linger on the goblin bit. Nope, not going there, I didn't have time to process it.

A spatter of laughter followed the Bro's pronouncement, followed by the sound of feet running from the scene. Four hulking figures stepped out of the shadows, surrounding the kid on the ground. These were not eighteen-year-old students—the maze had revealed its first challenge.

I smelled Pete before he reached me, a faint musk. I crinkled my nose. A heavy breath escaped him. "That's a goblin," he whisper-gasped. "The thugs there can deal with him. We can slip by, use him for distraction like the others did."

Wally—only a second behind Pete—nodded. "That plan will give us the best chances of survival, easily increasing our odds by seventy-five percent."

Sure, if we wanted to sacrifice someone to save ourselves.

I didn't work like that. I wasn't leaving the kid to those thugs. Goblin or not, he didn't deserve this. "You two slip by first, I'll follow and cover the rear." They didn't have to know what I was planning.

Wally crept ahead, pinning her back to the side of the building. Her eyes widened as she hit the edge of the light thrown by that single flickering lamp. Her entire body was visible to the thugs, but their eyes were on the small kid who'd tucked his body around himself, pressing against the wall like he hoped to disappear into it.

No doubt he'd thought he'd be safe going in with a big group of guys. But they hadn't lured their bait in the same way the girls ahead of them had. They'd flat out taken him with them, promising him safety in numbers.

Anger snapped up and through me. It was one thing to lure stupids after you, another to make a false promise of safety to someone who trusted you.

I motioned for Freckles to go, and he stepped surprisingly light on his feet, following Wally.

There was a thud of a boot hitting a body. I couldn't wait for Pete to get all the way across.

Sorry, bud.

I stepped into the light. "Y'all are pretty tough, huh, beating up on one kid? Four against, one? Really?" Pete squeaked, clearly visible to the four oversized thugs as they did a slow turn in unison.

I'd like to say in that moment I wasn't afraid, that I didn't take half a step back, that I didn't consider my poor life choices, including that one, in a single flash, but that would be a lie. The thugs…they didn't have faces. I mean like nothing. No eyes. No lips. Nothing, just a blank canvas of pasty white with weird stringy hair that hung past where ears should be. These creatures were not people, not even close to human.

Terror tripped along my spine and it made my mouth do terrible things.

"You got a felt marker? I could draw you in some eyebrows. Nice big bushy ones." I grinned through the fear, feeling the wild in me surge up and out.

Reckless, I know.

The one *thing* closest to me lifted a hand that held a short knife. I mimicked him. "You'd make amazing mimes. Like fantastic. Probably make a lot of money if you took your show on the road. You'd conquer one curb at a time."

"I'm going to pee my pants," Pete squeaked.

The knife-wielding faceless *thing* lunged at me, knife in a straight thrust for my guts. I danced to the side and swung a slice of my own with my blade, cutting across its arm. I grimaced as the blade dug into bone. A spurt of blood was sure to follow with a blow. Great gushes of it. Or something, there should have been something.

I yanked my knife back and the thug didn't slow, not for a split second, nor was there a single splatter of red.

Another of the hulking creatures went for Pete. I cut the thing off, knifing it where the kidney *should* be. It swung to face me, and I dropped to a knee, rolling out of the way.

Pete—bless his stupid heart—jumped into the fray. With their backs to him, the creatures didn't see him coming.

"I'll get this one, Billy!" he yelled as he *climbed* up the back of the brute closest to him. I couldn't help but stare.

How in the heck had he done that? Like he'd had handholds on the back of the—thing. I needed to understand what I was dealing with if I was going to beat them.

"Wally, what are they?" I yelled as I stepped closer to one of the creatures and kicked out, smashing my boot into the inside of its knee. The crunch was solid, and on a person would have shattered the bones, displacing the knee cap and rendering them pretty much useless. Not so much here. The beastie barely bobbled on its legs.

"Golems," Wally called out. "Anthropomorphic creatures made entirely from inanimate matter. They are controlled by their creator from a safe distance. Less than point-zero-zero-one percent of deaths have been caused by golems. But, to be fair, all of those deaths occurred within the Culling Trials."

Of course, they had.

Wally paused. "They are Jewish of origin if that helps."

"It does *not*!" I yelled as I ducked a knife swipe at my head. "Unless one of you is Jewish and knows what to do?"

Neither of them answered, which said it all.

"I got this one!" Pete yelped as he wrapped his arms around the neck of the golem he'd climbed, letting his legs swing out wide.

It was quite the sight. The rodeos at home had nothing on this.

"Fantastic info, Wally, but how do we stop them?" I dodged a big boot coming my way, straight for my head.

They were bendy bastards for being so big. The blow meant for my face missed so narrowly I could feel the wind slap my cheek.

"You don't kill them," the goblin kid on the ground said. "You leave them someone to torment while you continue on. That is how this works."

"Not today it doesn't," I said as I slid between the golems, keeping them swinging, arms and feet going in all directions. If I got close enough, maybe I could get them to smash into each other. "Pete, get ready to bail."

I put myself between two of the golems, keeping my hands at my sides. "Come on, ugly boys, let's see what you've got."

They swung for my head at the same time, one from the right, one from the left, and I dropped to the ground just before they struck flesh. They crashed into each other with an enormous cracking bang, like Humpty Dumpty having a really bad day, and I scrambled across the ground to the kid still crouched against the wall. I glanced behind me. The two golems now lay on the ground flat on their backs, blocking the paths of the other two. Beautiful.

Pete had bailed and was nowhere to be seen. For the moment, we were good, but it wouldn't last. "Time to move."

The kid's eyes lifted to mine—huge, round eyes that

were totally out of proportion with the rest of his face. "Why are you doing this? Nobody helps in the Culling Trials."

I wasn't about to tell him that he reminded me of Billy. That if my little brother had come instead of me, he probably would have made the same mistake as this kid—he would have hooked up with the big boys, thinking he'd be safe with them.

No one would have saved Billy, but I could save this kid.

"Not the time." I grabbed him by the arm and swung him up onto my back. How many times had I done this same move with Sam? Hundreds. And he was far lighter than she was even now.

I dodged the now stumbling golems, driving a foot into the knees of the two still standing, slowing them down. They were freaky to look at, but slow and dumb. Not much of a challenge if you asked me.

"Run," I said to Pete and Wally as I took off, the new kid clinging to my back like an oversized monkey.

"They'll track us," Pete said. "Golems don't give up their prey easily."

"Doubt it." I shot back. "If this is a trial, then there will be something else up ahead of us. The golems," cripes, I could not believe I was saying that word as if it were real, "won't follow us far. Otherwise, there wouldn't be anything left here for the kids who come after us. We just have to get to the next obstacle as quickly as we can."

"That seems like a bad idea," the kid on my back said. "Quick is death in the Culling Trials."

"Well, moving slow wasn't doing you any good," I pointed out.

"Touché," he said. "My name is Gregory."

"Gregory goblin?" Pete snickered. "Did your parents think you were going to end up in a comic book?"

Gregory's hands drifted to the top of my collarbone as I jogged along, precariously close to the girls. That was not happening.

"Okay, ride's over." I let go of him, dropping him to the ground abruptly.

He yelped as he hit the pavement, rolled, and came to his feet.

"Dumb jerk," he snapped up at me as he dusted off clothes that were nicer than anything I'd ever had in my closet. Did goblins have money? Or style for that matter? Apparently so.

"Yeah, well, this jerk just saved your butt, *Gregory Goblin*," I said. I checked my ball cap, tugging the rim to make sure it was on good and tight. This whole acting, looking, and talking like a guy thing was a lot of work. And I kept forgetting about the part I was supposed to be playing, which didn't help.

"Um, Billy?" Pete said.

"Call me Wild," I replied without thinking.

"I think we have a new problem."

Of course, we did. I made a slow turn and let out a big breath as I took in the scene ahead of us. "Jesus Murphy on a limping donkey, do we ever."

CHAPTER 11

SCREAMS ERUPTED BACK the way we'd come, followed by the sound of distant thumps. The golems had forgotten about us, just as I'd predicted.

A whole new problem lay ahead in this city of death we were trapped in. My eyes locked on what I could only see as a wall of death and dismemberment.

I didn't mean figuratively either. The ground dipped easily ten feet into a hole that stretched the width of the alley from building to building. The ditch, if it could be called that, was six feet wide, and ended in a metal wall stretching up and out of sight into a bank of fog. It resembled an oversized chicken wire fence with large blades jutting out at random intervals, which would force an intrepid climber along a particular path. I blinked and the blades closest to the ground drew back and popped out somewhere else on the wall. A faint dusting of rain pattered down around us. Not fog, then. Clouds. Wet metal was a right bitch to climb, slippery and cold. I flexed my hands, already sizing up the best path to take, timing the emergence of the blades.

"Okay, so I've seen worse," I said.

The buzz of electricity cut through the air, and the hair along my arms stood as parts of the wall glowed blue, sizzling against the rain.

"Really?" Gregory said beside me, rubbing his arms. "You've seen worse?"

I was going to answer but was interrupted by a bellow of pain somewhere above us. Way above us.

Pete swallowed hard enough that it was audible.

"Falls equate for a sum total of over six hundred fifty thousand, five hundred twenty deaths a year. Globally, that is," Wally said softly, the fear in her voice palpable.

"I've seen worse. We can do this," I repeated, more for myself than the others. "If those ladies in black ahead of us could get through, then so can we."

"Those ladies in black," Gregory said, "are from some of the longest lines of assassins this world has ever seen."

"Then we need to figure out how they did it." I took a few steps toward the ditch. The marks on the edge showed fresh scuffs left by the Bros who'd jumped across, pushing hard to make the full six-foot leap. I frowned as I lowered my gaze to the base of the ditch. I crouched and put my hands on the lip of the ditch, feeling the marks, seeing others that weren't immediately visible if you were, say, running from the golems.

This challenge was like going through the most violent haunted house I'd ever thought possible. But it was a puzzle too—one with deadly stakes.

I wasn't about to tell the others that I kinda liked it.

My wrist vibrated and I glanced at the watch as a message flashed across it.

Getting passed is bad for your health.

"Did you just get that message too?" I looked up at the other three and they nodded in unison.

Which meant we had to go.

Gregory launched across the open space, covering it easily, and began to climb the wall, his words echoing my thoughts. "We have to move!"

Only we didn't have to move, at least, not in the direction he was going. Not if the marks under my hands were any indication. "That's not the way."

Pete all but danced at my side, his feet tapping out a rhythm.

"You gotta pee still?" I asked.

"Yeah, when I get nervous." And he just whipped it out and started to whizz right in front of me. Like I was one of the guys. Which, of course, I was supposed to be. Wally squeaked and spun her back to him.

"Not in the ditch, you idiot!" I shoved him on the hip, turning him away from the hole.

"Why not?" He looked over his shoulder at me.

I lowered myself along the edge of the ditch, avoiding the splash of piss. "Because it's where we're going."

Wally nodded and sidestepped him. "That's good. I don't think anyone has died in a ditch. At least, not that I know of."

I wanted to ask her about the first two world wars but refrained.

My feet landed on much softer ground, boots sinking down with my weight. Mud, liquid mud. It had better just be mud seeing as there were no cows around. Wally slid down the side of the ditch and landed with a sloppy splash, Pete next, and remarkably enough, even Gregory.

"Change your mind?"

"I hate climbing." He wouldn't make eye contact with me, which was fine. Let him keep his pride.

Pete grabbed my arm. "I can smell cotton candy perfume. One of the girls was wearing that. They did come down this way. But how did you know?"

I pointed at the faint depressions in the soft ground, wondering how he'd smelled anything over the heavy scent of earth…and urine. But he was right—now that he'd pointed it out, I could pick up a faint cotton candy scent.

"Footprints," I said. I'd only seen them once I'd crouched. Even then, if I hadn't taken a moment to process what I was seeing, I would have missed them. Just like everyone who'd leapt at the obvious path. "Let's go. I don't want anyone else figuring this out if we can help it. Gregory, give me your coat."

"What are you going to do with it? You're too big," Gregory said, but he did hand it over.

I pushed the three of them ahead of me and then used his coat to brush away the footprints we left behind as best I could. "Covering our tracks." It wasn't as good as tree branch, but it would do the job.

They stepped ahead as I swept the area. I had to trust that they wouldn't go too far—and they didn't. I bumped into them as I reached the end of my sweeping job. They'd gathered under an overhang of street that hid us from the open mouth of the ditch. Again, you wouldn't have seen the overhang or the tunnel until you were in the ditch. "What are you waiting for?"

"It's locked." Pete jangled something metallic.

I turned to see a five-foot-tall gate that led underground, and by the initial direction, under all the buildings. From the gate hung a brand new lock. Too fresh, too new. I would have laid money that the ladies in black ahead of us had locked the gate. I sighed. "Any of you picked locks before?" I had, but I felt someone else needed to step up and show off their skills. That's what this place was about, right?

Gregory nodded. "I have." He held up his hands,

showing off long, almost delicate looking fingers. "I'm quite good at it actually. I just need something to work with."

"Would a bobby pin work?" Wally asked.

Gregory nodded, and she pulled one from her hair. I wasn't sure it was even holding anything up. Almost like she'd decided to put a few bobby pins in for an emergency. Which, given how much she and Pete knew about the trials, was a distinct possibility.

"While Gregory works, tell me what you know about this school," I said.

Wally's eyes widened and the telltale spitting of electricity made me grab Gregory and pull him back as the blue light flickered across the metal grate. "Thanks."

"No problem." I let him go but didn't take my eyes from Wally. "Talk to me, Wally. And not about death."

She shrugged. "That will be difficult because the Academy of Shadowspell is death incarnate in many ways. There are five houses within the school. From top to bottom in terms of standing amongst the world and magical community, it is the House of Wonder, where magic and power are held as the highest objectives first. The House of Night, where darkness and the undead rule, second. The House of Claw, where animals and their masters stand shoulder to shoulder, third. The House of Shade, where the shadows cover those who deal in death.

Fourth, and the final house—"

"The House of Unmentionables," Gregory said as he flourished his hands at the now-open grate. "Of which goblins and other unmentionables are a part."

I eyed him up. "You don't look much like a goblin. More like an undersized Justin Bieber."

Gregory's lips curled upward. "We get uglier as we get older. And ugliness is prized in our culture. We leave beauty to those who would be blinded by it."

Pete leaned in to me. "So, you just insulted him."

I opened my mouth to apologize and then clamped it shut. That was not what a guy would do. No, a guy would rub that insult in.

"Well, Biebs, you're one cute little runt, aren't you?"

He opened his mouth, showing off rather sharp teeth and emitting an even sharper hiss, when the sound of voices reached us. The group behind us had almost caught up.

Without a word, the four of us hurried through the open grate and closed it softly behind us. I thought about locking the gate as those ahead of us had, but I wasn't that much of a jerk. If the others behind us figured out to get into the ditch, I wasn't going to slow them down. I left the padlock hanging so that it appeared to be locked but wasn't fully engaged.

I turned away to see Gregory watching me. Pete had

his nose in the air as he stepped farther into the underground tunnel.

"This way, I can smell that perfume. It makes me hungry," he said. Wally was next to him and I thought I heard her say something about death by perfume causing lungs to collapse.

A few steps in and my shoulders itched, right down the middle, a warning if ever I'd felt one. I turned to see Gregory watching me closely.

"What?" I asked.

"You are not…what I expect from a Shade," he said.

A frown pulled my lips down. "A shade?"

He pointed at my nametag. "They think you'll end up in the House of Shade based on your ancestry, though no one can be certain until after the sorting at the end of the Culling Trials." He shrugged. "No one else could have dodged the speed of those golems. Except maybe a vampire, but you're definitely not one of those."

There was a scuff behind us and I spun. Nothing but shadows. Still…maybe something was stalking us, even if I wasn't picking up any danger from that direction.

My frown deepened as I kept pace with Gregory in the rounded-out tunnel. Water sloshed under our feet and the faint scent of shit curled around us. Like we'd stepped into the sewer system under a big city. "The golems weren't that fast."

"They were a blur to me." Gregory said softly. "I could not have avoided them on my own."

That made no sense. "They were slow as turtles in molasses come February."

Gregory snorted. "That's my point. I couldn't see *you* either. The ability to move at speeds that can only be matched or beaten by a full vampire is the House of Shade personified."

I glanced at him then down at the tag on my chest. "And you're not just saying that because of this?"

Under my name was a single word. Shade.

Gregory looked ahead. "Even without it, I would know what you are. Your kind and mine often work closely, as we are considered…less than those with true magic."

I shrugged. "And if I am a Shade?"

"Then you are the only reason the other three of us will make it out of this trial alive and with any standing," he said.

"No pressure at all, right?" A dry laugh escaped me.

A moment later, we caught up with Pete and Wally, who'd stopped walking. It wasn't hard to see why—the tunnel bucketed out into open space. Wally had pressed herself against the rounded curve of the wall, and Pete leaned out over the opening on his hands and knees. "Holy cats, Wild. Check this out."

As Gregory and I stepped up to the lip of the tunnel, I got my first look at the next challenge.

"It looks like a video game," Pete said. "All those platforms, ladders, ropes, and lots and lots of places to fall. And how is it that tall? We aren't that far underground, are we?"

He wasn't wrong, but something wasn't right. "We've been walking downhill the last ten minutes, so yeah, it is possible." I thought for a moment. "Wally or Biebs, either of you get a feel for this place?"

Sure, Gregory thought I was made for this place, but that didn't mean I believed him. Even if I felt a flash of recognition deep in my belly that he was *not* wrong. Even if the emotion that coursed through me was nothing short of adrenaline-fueled excitement.

Gregory tipped his head. "Why are you asking me? Us?"

"It's smarter, that's why. The group as a whole is greater than its individual parts," I said. "So you got anything?"

Gregory wiggled his fingers and closed his eyes. Like he was communing with the dead or something, which at this point in my day I would not be surprised about. He gave a full body shiver and then nodded. "There's gold nearby. It's…" He pointed upward and vaguely ahead of us. "It's somewhere…above us. Other than that, I cannot be sure."

"My mother said that only the House of Shade people go for the gold," Pete said, shaking his head. "It's really hard to get. She said just to get through as fast as possible without taking any detours, but…I don't see a set path, do you?"

"What do you mean gold? The lady in the beginning said it was a bonus. Is it…like a medal?" I stared up at the oversized death trap, a plethora of circular platforms separated by empty space, connected by ropes or ladders here and there, although not enough of them.

"No, in each trial there is the opportunity to set yourself apart from the others," Gregory said. "You can complete the trial, or you can test yourself against a harder challenge and be rewarded financially. There is only one chance at the bonus per trial, so if one group gets it now, no one else will today. Then they ante-up another trunk of gold for the next run-through, so for each run, everyone has a chance. The actual amount of the bonus is determined by the house and can change. The shifters tend to put up more gold to *encourage* people, for example."

My eyes tracked along the bits and pieces as I considered what he was saying.

"Would the gold be on the way out, do you think?" I asked.

"It should be," Wally answered, "But it's got to be protected by something. They won't just hand you gold to keep. We'd have to fight for it."

"They handed us a bunch of cash to come here," I said.

"Yeah...but you *had* to come here," Pete said.

Touché.

A flash of movement up on the course caught my attention.

One of the ladies in black who'd entered the trial ahead of us leapt from one platform to another, her long blonde hair floating behind her. She was aiming for a smaller platform diagonally right, in the general direction Gregory had pointed.

"How would she know where the gold is?" I said softly, scanning the course again, trying to discern any identifying markers. Because it was clear she was purposefully heading to a rope leading into the mists. She didn't have a goblin on her back, so something in the course must've clued her in.

"You get more points if you get the gold," Wally said.

"Wait." I held up my hand. "There's a point system for the trials?"

"Yes," she answered like I was dense.

I grinned. "So if we get all the gold, and those ladies in black don't, we win?"

"Well, yes…or we die trying. Which isn't a great option," Pete said.

"We also get to keep the gold," Gregory said with a hunger in his voice that I understood. Growing up poor, the pull of money was strong. The ability to send it home to my dad and the twins was worth the chance.

"No one outside of the House of Shade has ever walked away with the gold," Wally said. "Those that try usually fail the whole course."

I rubbed my hands together, something in me feeling the challenge and wanting to meet it head on. Percentages meant nothing to me. "First time for everything, Wally. First time for everything. Besides, it's a sure way out."

Pete sighed like a man completely spent. "I should've never followed you in here. It's going to get me killed."

Why I grinned, I couldn't say.

I leapt out from the lip of the tunnel onto the floating platform closest to me.

CHAPTER 12

I HAVE TO admit, there was a large part of me that was worried about this next part of the trial. What if I was leading the others the wrong way? What if I was wrong? It would not be the first time I'd led others into danger—I'd done it before with Tommy and Rory. Anxiety rocketed through me, but it was too late, I was already in the air.

The platform swayed under my feet, jarred from my sudden transfer of weight. I moved to the edge and turned, bracing as Wally jumped after me. The woman had no fear, though muttering to herself was certainly an issue. She was probably recounting the likelihood of her imminent death.

"Running, jumping, math—this has become my personal Vietnam," Pete said before gearing up and taking a running start. When his jump peaked too far away from the platform, his eyes rounded.

He wasn't going to make it.

"Hold my legs, Wally." I pushed forward and

stretched out a hand.

Pete's arms windmilled like he was a cartoon character. "I'm going to die!" he screeched.

"Reach out, you blockhead," I hollered, straining forward.

The fingers on his right hand brushed mine. His left hand swung around as he lost altitude. "I'M FALLING! I'M FALLING!"

Adrenaline and fear dumped into my body, the space below us sucking up my focus. If he missed, he'd have a long fall before he went splat.

His palm slapped my wrist and slid. I curled my fingers, dimpling his skin so I wouldn't lose hold of him, and slammed my other hand down on his forearm.

"Don't…go into…hysterics, just hang on," I said in a series of grunts, my body sliding toward the edge with the weight.

Wally's fingers, stronger than I would've expected, tightened on my ankles and anchored me to the platform. My forward progress halted, but Pete's weight tore at me and I fought to hang on to him. He swung under the platform before slamming into something solid.

"Ow," he said.

"You would not believe the amount of deaths that occur each year from blunt force trauma," Wally mumbled. I needed to find her off switch.

"Hang on, buddy," I said, pulling on his arm with all my strength. "I got you."

"Don't drop me." Pete reached up with his other arm, grasping both of mine.

Gregory flew through the air, his feet *thunking* down next to me, too close for comfort. He dropped and rolled past before springing up and crawling back.

"I guess if you're hellbent on saving him, I can help," Gregory drawled before crowding in.

"Yes. Please. Be hellbent on saving me. Please," Pete said in a high-pitched, terrified voice. He wasn't great at staying calm in near-death situations.

Gregory reached down over the platform and took hold of Pete's arms. He pulled with me, our combined strength enough to drag Pete over the lip of the platform.

"Holy cats," Pete said as he scrambled up. "That was close."

"One of many close calls to come," Wally said. I sure hoped that wasn't her idea of comfort.

Breathing heavily, confident that Pete would be fine, I dusted myself off and turned to survey the way ahead. In the distance, four lithe shapes, dressed in black, climbed a rope from the target platform before disappearing into the swirling mists above.

"One is missing," I said quietly, searching the platforms for any other movement. "Five set out, but only four are up there." The Bro Pack was nowhere to be seen. Across from us was an opening in the wall, and I suspected they'd taken the easy way out.

"Maybe she fell," Pete said, stepping up beside me. "Though the rest of them are getting up that rope really fast."

"Forget them, how are we going to get to that platform?" Gregory said, his tone dubious. "It's a maze, only instead of walls, it has huge gaps. We can't jump a ton of those."

I turned my focus to the course, taking stock of the layout, the various sized platforms, and most importantly, the gaps. Almost immediately, it became apparent that there was only one manageable path to the target platform and it was long, complex, and windy. More than one jump gave me pause, a few platforms looked like they might not be stationary, and the swinging rope near the end almost made me throw in the towel and aim for the easier exit point.

But those girls had made it. Clearly, it was possible.

"I can get us there," I said confidently.

"Are you sure?" Pete said. "Every path I pick out ends in a ginormous gap."

"She's a Shade," Wally replied. "She's good at strategy and puzzles and stuff. We follow her, and we'll make it."

It's true. I was good at puzzles. The best in my family

actually. No one would play chess with me anymore.

"I can get us there, but there will be a couple hairy spots." I chewed my lip, cutting my eyes to Pete. "This will need to be a group effort. I need you all to commit."

Wally and Gregory joined me in looking at Pete, clearly the weak link when it came to jumping the gaps. Pete nodded, either not catching our dubious looks or finding his courage within them.

"I can do it," Pete said, determination overshadowing the uncertainty in his voice.

I nodded once, no more than a jerk of my head, and jogged forward before leaping to the next platform. Once I touched down, I turned and pointed. "Wally, you next. Then Gregory. Brace yourself near the edge and wait for Pete. Good?"

"Okay," Wally called mid-jump, landing in the center of the platform and bumping into me. Gregory landed without a hitch this time, careful not to touch us, before Pete flung himself in with wide eyes and wildly swinging arms.

Thankfully, Pete did get better as we made our way, and amazingly, handled the swinging rope like a champ, only bungling his landing on the small platform.

All of us breathing heavy, we congregated two platforms away from the target, the others quietly letting me assess where to go next. They'd only questioned me once on the way up, Gregory thinking one of the chosen platforms would lead us to a dead end. My explanation had been quick and distracted as I recalled the way forward, but strangely, it had been enough to appease them all. After that, they'd followed blindly. We were making good time, so I wasn't complaining.

A strange feeling washed over me. Shivers of warning coated my skin and cold crept up my spine. I glanced around, trying to pierce the darkening haze suddenly pressing in on us with my gaze. Something was out there, waiting. Watching. It wasn't the something that had been dogging me either. Whatever this was, it meant us harm.

A new urgency pushing me on, I leapt to the next platform. The wood under my feet swung forward with my weight. I windmilled my arms with the sudden shift in balance and barely kept from toppling backward into open air. This hadn't looked like a swinging platform.

"Careful on this one," I said with a shaking voice, crouching to stabilize.

"Wow." Wally let out a breath and clutched her chest. "That was a close one. I thought you were going over."

So had I.

"It's too far now," Pete called as I surveyed the swirling mists rolling and drifting above the knotted rope hanging down to the target platform.

A glance back said he was right. The platform wasn't

a swinging platform after all. It had shifted under my weight, and it hadn't drifted back. Which meant…

"You're all on your own on this one," I said, making the easy leap to the target platform. As expected, the platform I'd been on drifted back to its default position, close enough for one of the others to jump. "There is no safety net."

"It's like watching a master at work," Wally said, a cockeyed grin on her face. "Isn't it? I mean, wow."

"That's why the Sandman was escorting him, I told you," Pete replied. "I really hope I don't fall. My worst fear is falling like this. I thought I was a goner when I fell out of the chopper earlier. That was a mean trick to just let students slide out."

My talent with strategy and life-sized puzzle games wasn't why the Sandman had taken an interest in me, but I let it lie. The less they knew about why I was there, the better.

The warning from a moment ago intensified until a feeling of dread seeped into my bones. My chest tightened and heart sped up. Something was coming. Something dangerous to all of us.

I shifted my weight back and forth, needing to move. To run or fight. But I didn't know what form the threat would take. And there was nowhere to run *to*.

"Let's get going," I called out as Wally made the

jump. "Fast as we can."

Pete rolled his shoulders and looked around him, standing next to Gregory. "Do you feel that?" he asked Gregory as an itch manifested right between my shoulder blades.

Gregory ignored him, watching as Wally made the final leap to me and the target platform, graceful now that she knew the platform moved. Moments later, she landed next to me.

"Eyes." Pete turned in a circle. "It feels like we're being watched." He lifted his nose, sniffing the air.

Sweat broke out on my forehead and I turned to the rope, knotted for ease of climbing, leading up into those dark gray, almost black, swirling mists.

"What do you think is up there?" Wally asked quietly.

"Trouble," I said, yanking on the rope a little, just to make sure it was really attached to something.

Gregory jumped onto the target platform with us, leaving the other one to drift back to hopefully collect Pete.

"Careful, it moves," Wally reminded him.

"This rope is too easy to climb," I said softly, thinking through all of this. "The path here was complex. Getting here was physically taxing. And now, at the endgame, it's a knotted rope? Why not just make it a ladder?"

"How else would we get up?" Wally asked, confused.

"She means it's too easy," Gregory said, quickly drowned out by a screaming Pete.

"Made it," Pete yelled, squatting like an attack spider. "I made it."

"It's too easy," I agreed.

"I smell the gold," Gregory said, his gaze arcing skyward. "It's faint and kind of fluctuating, like it's being carried on a breeze, but it's closer now."

"I really wish I could smell gold," Wally said wistfully. "But I don't feel a breeze."

I shook my head. Neither did I.

"Easy or not, this is the way up." I curled my fingers around the rope.

Pete yelled out a curse when his platform stopped moving, but thankfully didn't pitch off the edge. Shaky, he jumped to meet us.

"Bad news, Pete," I said, not able to tear my eyes away from those swirling mists. Everything in me said the danger lay up there. That to climb this rope would put our lives at stake. But hadn't that been the case with the other challenges thus far? In jumping across the large gaps?

No. This is different.

I pushed my strange certainty away. It wasn't helping. But I knew without a doubt that I needed to send the others up first—I just didn't know why.

"You should go first," I said to Pete. "That mist up there is probably fifty feet up, and who knows what's beyond it. If you suddenly lose your grip, we should probably have someone to stop you from going splat. Besides, you seem to have a knack for climbing."

"I hate this," Pete said, ambling over.

"Yes, but when we get to your house's trial, we'll all probably hate that." Wally patted Pete on the back. "It'll be even then."

Pete gave a little hop, hefting himself up onto the rope. A strange vibration drifted through me, like ripples in a dark pond.

You don't belong here, it seemed to say. *You will go no farther.*

I hadn't felt that when I'd touched the rope, only when Pete had.

I ripped my gaze higher, the itch between my shoulder blades turning into claws scratching and digging in deep. The angry mists swirled above. Something unseen looked down through them. I was certain.

"Watch yourself on the other side of those mists," I said to Pete, stepping closer. "Get up, fast as possible, but keep your eyes peeled." I dragged my bottom lip through my teeth. "This might've been a bad idea."

"These are the Culling Trials," Wally said, pushing in behind me. "You'd be hard pressed to find a good idea if it means staying out of danger."

Hand over hand, Pete pulled himself up, his feet finding awkward placement about as often as they missed.

"Wally, you next. Go." I shoved her at the rope, not waiting for Pete to get too far.

Gregory didn't wait for my direction. He must've sensed I'd want to go last, to catch anyone who fell.

A scream rent the vast silence of the platform area behind us. I spun around as the rest of the crew stopped climbing, craning their necks to look over their shoulders.

Four people scattered from the lip of the tunnel, rushing for the sides, hands reaching for something to hang on to so they didn't join their friend.

"He was pushed," one of them shouted, looking behind him. "I swear to Christ, he was pushed!"

"Go." I shoved at Gregory's butt. "Go!"

"Colt, did you see who did it?" one of the other guys asked.

Another said, "Better him than us."

Light flared from the end of a stick in a muscular guy's hand. It shot into the air, illuminating the area in hazy red light.

I used the opportunity to look up through the swirling dark mists at the top of the rope. There, just above Pete, lying on her stomach with her upper body slung over the side of a platform was the lady in black with blonde hair. Her hand moved in a sawing motion and the knife she held glinted in the throbbing reddish light.

"She's cutting the rope," I yelled, helplessly throwing up my finger.

Her gaze flicked from her task to me, and in that look, I saw sparkling cunning. She was enjoying the game, and sabotaging fellow trial goers was part of the fun.

"Climb faster than you've ever climbed before," I yelled at Pete even as someone from the tunnel shouted, "That black widow is trying to throw the trial!"

I turned in time to see a blast shoot out from the guy's stick, what I had to finally admit was a wand capable of real magic. A jet of bright blue light streaked through the air. It passed within feet of the girl cutting the rope and she jerked away, rolling to the side.

I looked for something to throw. Anything.

"Go, Pete," Wally yelled. "Go, Pete!"

"I'm hurrying," he said, his movements jerky and his breath short. "I'm hurrying." Another jet of light cut through the air, screaming by me. The heat coated my arm.

"It's not us," I yelled, taking hold of the rope as my crew labored up. "We're not—"

A dark shape moved behind one of the guys at the lip

of the tunnel.

"Look out—" I screamed, but it was too late. He pitched forward, his hands clutching the air as his feet left solid ground. Although he had a wand, it didn't help him any. Light erupted from the end, slicing through the air and exploding against the earth ceiling far above our heads. He screamed, reaching for a platform that was too far away, but gravity took hold, and his body dropped from view.

"Hurry up," one of the guys shouted, an attractive man with confidence and swagger in spades.

Soft laughter echoed down in the failing red light, and I could just barely see the blonde girl, still leaning out over my crew. She winked, setting off warning bells…and then she was gone.

"This is what happens when the mean girls get free rein," I said through suddenly numb lips, grabbing the rope.

"The mean girls are nothing," Wally said as Pete ascended through the fog. "It's the murderous bastards you have to look out for. In the Culling Trials, they don't have leashes."

"Clearly."

Down to three, the guys behind us took to the platforms. The muscular one, tall and broad, with a wave of dirty blond hair, swept his wand in front of him. Footprints shimmered into existence on three of the platforms—the first three we'd taken. He followed in our footsteps, literally, leading the other guys. When he got to the furthermost one, he stopped and waved his wand again.

"Cheater," I grumbled. "Let's hustle, everyone. They're able-bodied. They'll be here in no time."

"I'm surprised he doesn't have a map," Pete said in a strained voice, clearly recognizing the guy. "Crap. Oh crap, what's that… It sounds like something is groaning."

"It's the rope," Wally said, fear riding her words. "It's the rope. The rope is going to break. Hurry up, Pete. And no more Snickers bars. No more. You're officially cut off."

"I'm at the top," Pete yelled a moment later. "I'm there!"

"Then pull yourself up," Gregory shouted.

The guys behind us were only a few platforms away by the time I reached the deep cut in the rope. As I pulled myself over it, a second strand broke free, pulling hard on the remaining strand. I doubted it would hold strong for the copycats, at least not all three.

"It's that way," Gregory was saying as I heaved myself up over the lip of the wooden platform at the top.

On the left, a shaky looking suspension bridge hung over nothingness, leading to another tunnel. Gregory pointed in the opposite direction, across a log with no handrails suspended over a sea of spikes. The end of the log disappeared into more dark, swirling mists, this trial clearly using the unknown to spark fear into our hearts.

A small table on the log side of the platform held three pairs of binoculars and large metallic discs that I figured were shields.

"Those spikes are an illusion," Pete said, drifting closer. "Right? Or else there would've been a strip of roof above some of the platforms, and there wasn't. It was all one big, open cavern."

"So, it's an illusion, so what?" Gregory picked a set of the binoculars. "If we don't fall on spikes, we'll bust our heads on the platforms way below. Not a big difference."

"The number of people—"

"No." Pete held his hand up for Wally. "Don't say it. Whatever horrible stat it is, don't say it. I don't want to know."

The rope groaned behind me. The dirty blond, muscular guy had just started up, one of his friends joining him a moment later.

"We're out of time."

Gregory sucked in a breath through his teeth. "There it is," he said, cutting me off. "Holy shi—"

"Lemme see." Pete grabbed a set of the binoculars. "Oh f—I changed my mind. I'm in. Gold. I choose gold."

I took the two quick steps and grabbed the last pair of binoculars. They cut through the mist, revealing a doorway and a room beyond it. I sucked in my own breath as an enormous pile of gleaming gold caught my attention. It sat atop a stout table in front of the rear door, spilling down onto the floor there was so much of it.

"Holy crap," I said softly, but I couldn't let the gold blind me to the danger. There was a reason they'd provided shields. I swung the binoculars to the right, at the ivy-covered wall in the distance. There, on a wide platform with a door at his back, a bow in his lap and a quiver of arrows at his side, sat none other than Sideburns, his own binoculars pressed to his eyes.

I gave him a wave featuring one of my fingers. He'd gotten me into all this, he deserved a little shade thrown his way. Pun intended.

On the other side, much closer, a woman leaned against the cavern wall. A metal stand with six holes, each filled with long sticks, took up a large portion of her deep platform.

"Silly, rabbit," I muttered to myself, zooming in on the stand beside her. Then I chuckled to myself, because what the hell else could I do? "Those aren't sticks, they're spears."

"What's that?" Gregory said.

Something snapped and a scream filled the air. A loud *thunk* cut off the sound.

I spun, finding the dirty blond man just climbing over the wooden platform. Once up, he took a quick look down, his demeanor unaffected by whatever he saw.

"Did that rope snap?" I asked, hurrying over.

"You don't want to see." Wally held up her hand to stop me, looking over the edge. "Unless you like a leg bent the wrong way. Then you do want to see."

"Colt is tough; he'll be fine." The blond guy stepped away from the edge, giving Wally a wide berth. The untrustworthy rarely trusted those around them. "This is it, then? This is the path to the Shade treasure? How much are they offering?"

Gregory and Pete backed away as the blond guy sauntered toward the log, his eyes scanning the shields before he reached out for the binoculars.

I held onto them. He hadn't said please.

"What have we got?" the guy said, looking my way when his hand wasn't immediately filled with the binoculars.

"A party crasher," I growled low, my guard up. I tugged my hat a little lower, and wiped a hand across my cheek, smearing sweat and a good amount of mud still there from the ditch.

The dirty blond guy turned toward me, his eyes bluer

than any eyes had a right to be. He took my measure for one solid beat, but this wasn't the way a man would usually size up a woman, analyzing her face for beauty before looking at her body—he puffed up slightly, pushing out his chest and leaning in just a little, a play for dominance.

Because, of course, I was a dude.

I liked this far better. Beauty I couldn't control, but kicking him in the head to prove my dominance was well within my skill level.

Stare hard and body loose, I met his gaze and held it. I didn't want to care what he looked like, but there was nothing wrong with my eyesight. His face was classically handsome—straight nose, defined jaw, and high cheekbones. The set of his robust body and broad shoulders denoted a level of confidence above average, and the upward tilt of his face and superior air led me to believe he'd grown up affluent, not rough and tumble like I had. I hadn't met many people like that, but there was no mistaking the cloud of entitlement.

That meant he hadn't learned street smarts the hard way. He hadn't needed to. That gave me an edge he would never understand.

I smirked and handed over the binoculars, secure in my place at the top of the pile. In response, his brow lowered in obvious confusion. He'd catch on sooner or later. In the meantime, we could use him. He was good with that wand, even if his aim could use some work.

"Arrows on the right, spears to the left," I said, turning toward the log. "At the end is a plain room that surely houses all sorts of nightmares. There's no way they'd be content to give away all that gold to someone with good balance and quick feet."

Mr. Peepers lifted the binoculars to his eyes, checking my findings. A moment later, he blew out a breath. "Crap. That's the Sandman."

"Oh, you recognize the sideburns, do you?"

"Good balance and quick feet won't be enough against him," he said.

"That's why they've given us shields, I'd imagine." I dragged my lip through my teeth and glanced back at the suspension bridge. "Did those girls try their hand, do you think?"

"Which girls?" Peepers rolled his finger across the top of the binoculars, zooming in as he looked at the room across the way.

"The five girls that went down the path first. I saw four of them make it to this platform."

Peepers took the binoculars away and studied me for a moment. "Did one of the girls cut the rope, or did you stage that?"

"Hard to cut a rope when you're still climbing it."

His brows lowered. “For a no magic hack, yeah, I guess.” The binoculars clattered across the table—he clearly had no respect for someone else’s property. “If they went this way, they didn’t make it far, being that the gold is still there. The spikes are an illusion. If they fell, they landed wherever the losers go. The arrows and spears are real, though. Those’ll hurt. They won’t aim to kill, so the worst thing you’ll face is falling or pain.” He glanced around at our motley crew. “Only one question left. Who’s going first?”

CHAPTER 13

A LOG OVER an open chasm, spikes waiting to stick you from below, and two shooters working to knock you into said spikes. This was not a good idea.

"Wait, wait, wait." I held up both hands, connecting eyes with Wally, Pete, and then Gregory. Whatever my own inclinations, I had to consider their safety—no different than if it were Billy and Sam with me. "Look, this is incredibly dangerous. What are the chances we'll get that gold?"

Pete looked at Wally. "Well?"

"I..." She put out her hands. "I don't have enough information to calculate that. Not good?"

"Oh sure. When we really need it, where are you?" Pete asked.

"What are you, chicken?" Peepers taunted me, and I got the feeling that line was supposed to pack more punch than it did.

I ignored him. "Crossing that log will be hard enough, but whatever's in that room will probably be nuts. Or we could just take the suspension bridge out of here. With the rope cut, no one else will get that gold. We'll still get a win, the ladies in black didn't take the gold, that much is obvious. We'll get out of this trial. I know it."

"I'll get that gold," Peepers said confidently.

I waved my hand at the log. "Well then, be my—"

"No, wait." Pete stepped forward. "Bi—Wild, wait. You go. You go first."

"What?" I widened my eyes. Talk about throwing someone to the wolves.

Wally's voice took on the tone that had earned her the nickname. "Cheaters never prosper unless those cheaters are from the Helix family."

Peepers huffed out a laugh. "What sort of freak show did I walk into? Look, are you going to go, or what? It might be helpful to see how you're taken out. Otherwise, step aside."

Pete skulked over to me, his back bowed and head low, showing submission, though not to me. To Peepers.

"He gets everything handed to him, Wild," Pete said quietly. "His dad probably told him exactly how to beat this challenge. What spells to use, who to follow, who to knock out first. We can't let him have it. You can do it. You don't even have to cheat, you're so dang good. You should get the money, not him."

"What happened to 'we'?" I mumbled as Peepers bent for a closer look at the log, pushing it with one toe.

"We'll keep him from taking you out when you reach for the gold," Pete said out of the side of his mouth. He jerked his head, and I saw that Gregory was eyeing Peepers in obvious disdain.

"Who is he?" I asked as a shock of anxiety rolled through me, followed by a surge of excitement. Crossing that log would be no problem—I'd crossed the creek on our property via logs, rocks, and any manner of bridge more times than I could count, in all sorts of conditions. Being shot at was one of those conditions if you counted rocks, sling shots, paintballs, and once a dead possum. As the youngest of our crew growing up, and the only girl, I was often the odd man out. I'd always been elected to play the role of the enemy—I got good at avoiding rapid fire.

But none of that would help me with whatever waited in the room at the end. That was a giant blind spot. Despite the obvious danger, I was eager to test myself against it. If I didn't have to drag the others into my bad decisions with me, I could do so guilt-free.

"He's Ethan Helix, Bruce Helix's son," Pete said, then waited expectantly.

My shaking head wasn't what he was looking for.

"*Bruce* Helix." Another expectant pause and wide

eyes. "Cripes, do you know anything about the magical world?"

"I didn't even know there was one," I said.

He rolled his eyes in disbelief. "He runs the North American branch of Shadowlight. Super powerful, connected, rich, and his family goes back centuries in the magical world. He's a big deal. Like *the* big deal."

"Usually, the big deals are the biggest blowhards."

Pete leaned in close. "He's a blow hard with a lot of clout. Helix always wins, Wild. His family, I mean. They are always on top. If just once, someone else…" His words trailed away, and I heard him loud and clear.

Just once it would be nice if the little guy won. If the underdog took home the prize.

I nodded, determination raging through me. "Let's see how a farm gi—boy—from Nowhere, Texas stacks up against the big dog, shall we?"

Pete's smile stretched from ear to ear.

"Ladies and gentlemen," Wally said in her strangely deep voice. "Hold onto your seats. The show is about to begin."

"What is with that voice?" Ethan said, looking at Wally.

"I'll go first." I strutted up to the table beside the log, letting the thrill of the moment energize me. If I hurried, I wouldn't have time to think about the obvious differences between the creek at home and this log suspended above either sharp spikes or absolutely nothing for hundreds of feet, depending on how you looked at it. I wouldn't reflect on the vastly different pain potential of a well-placed arrow or spear versus a paintball or roadkill. And I certainly wouldn't think about the death trap at the other end with its hidden dangers just waiting to snap closed on me.

Nope, best to just keep moving.

I hefted a shield, gauging the weight. Not terribly heavy, and while I held it, it also seemed to lighten a little. I grabbed another, knowing I'd need two. There was no way I could pivot and turn to use only one shield on the log—I'd need to brace with a shield on each side.

Adrenaline coursed through me as I eyed the log again.

"Fortune favors the brave," I mumbled, using Rory's favorite catchphrase growing up.

"What a circus," Ethan mumbled.

I placed one foot solidly on the log and shifted my weight. No give. I slid it out a little farther. Still nothing. The log was solid.

"Here we go." I stepped out with the second foot as Wally put the binoculars to her eyes.

"Our hero steps onto the log," she said in her newsroom voice.

"Don't look down," Pete called out.

I gritted my teeth, ignoring the urge to do just that.

Eyes straight, I let my mind relax and focused on feeling the log under my feet. Trusting its solidity and my balance. A slight breeze slid across my skin before a prickle of warning brushed down my right side.

Wally's voice drifted into my calm, announcing an incoming arrow from the right.

I took a step to align my body before bending, ducking down between the shields. As tall as I was, they didn't cover everything. The arrow sliced through the air right behind my head. Had I not taken that step and ducked, it would've given me a new ear hole.

Apparently killing was a *go*. Sideburns didn't pull any punches. I guess his pep talk didn't prevent him from going for the jugular. Then again, had he pulled any so far? Not really. Besides, there was that incident with me shoving him and his car in the ditch. Probably made him look bad.

"Wally," I called out as a trickle of warning slid down my left. "I need you to announce kill zones. Head height, chest height, stomach, so on."

"You got it, boss—"

"Chest, chest, chest, chest, *chest*!" Pete called out.

I held firm and a spear clanged off of my shield, pushing my weight too far right. I surged up and pushed forward, needing movement to regain my balance. Another warning lit up my right side.

"Right. Legs," Wally called out as Pete sounded the same alarm in a much higher pitch.

I took two fast steps, focusing again on the solid log beneath my feet. On my balance. On sensing which sides the blows would come from. Having regained my focus, I crouched between the shields. The arrow zipped past me. Sideburns hadn't expected my movements and he was too far away to react in time to erratic changes. Good news for me.

"Left, chest," Pete called out.

I pushed to walking, his warning—and a prickle from the left—giving me enough time to brace for impact. As expected, the spear rammed into my shield, mighty in power. I faltered, my weight thrown, needing a moment to get my bearings. But a new threat was already coming in.

"Right, legs," Wally called urgently. "Right, head. Right, arm. *Run*!"

On impulse, I spun and took two fast steps—back the way I'd come. Shield at body height, an arrow clipped the very edge. The others missed, but not by much. I swiveled back around. Hurrying now, I kept my focus on the solid log. On my balance. Trusting in my ability. Staying calm.

"Good one," Pete called.

"She's readying two," Gregory hollered. "Left. She's readying two."

"The Sandman has his bow lowered," Wally said. "Not sure why."

"He's watching his prey, that's why," I said to myself, not wanting to advertise. Then, louder, "Keep me updated on what they're doing."

"Roger," Wally called.

"She's throwing," Pete said. "Two, one in each hand. Holy crap, is she ambidextrous?"

"Body, body," Gregory called.

I put on more speed, nearing the center of the log at a fast walk.

"Impact!" Pete shouted.

The spears hit the edge of my shield—the first with the expected force, and the second compounding it.

I swore under my breath and, not hearing Wally, took a second to pause and regain my headspace. I let out a slow breath, but before I could fully release it, Wally was announcing, "He's getting ready—rapid-fire, rapid-fire!"

"Where?" I shouted, but it was too late. The first arrow whistled an inch from the tip of my nose as I dropped down, crouching between my shields. Another sliced across the back of my neck. Pain blossomed, and I grimaced as third arrow sailed overhead and a fourth struck my shield.

He was covering all his bases, forcing me down.

As if hearing my thoughts, Gregory yelled, "Go, go, go, go!"

I didn't wait to be told twice.

"Here comes another one," Pete shouted. "Left! Left! I mean, body!"

That's all she did, the spear thrower—her might was the weapon. Her might made me go into defense mode, where Mr. Sunshine and his barrage of arrows could pick me off.

"Adapt, damn it," I scolded myself. "You know what they're doing. Adapt and get off this log!"

I walked at a fast clip, steady, seeing the blur from the left out of the corner of my eye. As the spear neared, I turned just a little and angled the shield. The spear ricocheted off, some of the impact deflected.

"Rapid-fire, rapid-fire," Wally shouted. "All over. Up, down—"

I hurried forward, half running, my gaze on the log and the shield covering my vitals. Searing pain sliced through my calf before vibrating up my body. Metal arrow tips clattered off the shield.

The mist cleared slowly as I neared the end, the door jiggling in my vision. An arrow point jostled my hat and I jerked, lifting the shield. My balance wavered. I crouched and took a deep breath to stabilize myself, thinking of the spikes below me. Thinking of the long plummet after they dissipated to nothingness.

"Left. Wait, she—left! She's throwing!" Pete shouted.

I surged up, my heart in my throat, not completely balanced but clearly out of time. The spear smacked the shield, the impact vibrating my arm but not shoving me as hard. I was farther away now, she'd missed her chance. The arrow-slinging lunatic, however, was plenty close.

"Rapid-fire, rapid-fire," Wally shouted again, and I swung my left shield to my right side, stacking them on top of each other to cover my whole body. The weight of the two compounded, dragging me close to the edge. I breathed as slowly as I could and focused on the log under my feet. On balance.

Metal dinged off metal, the arrows smacking the shields so fast, my mouth dropped open. I couldn't believe someone could shoot and reload that quickly, from that distance, and continuously hit their mark.

"Left," Pete yelled. "Body."

I switched the left shield back with effort. My breath coming in fast in gulps as my stamina was tested. An arrow smacked into my boot, not forceful enough to pierce the leather. Pain flared across my knee and I sucked in a surprised gasp. Another arrow sliced through my pants, opening a gash in the back of my thigh. I staggered as yet another spear smashed into the left shield, throwing my weight too far right.

I tried to windmill my arms, so close to the edge I could almost jump. But the shields hampered me and the pain shooting up my leg stopped me from dancing forward to get my bearings. Pete yelled, Wally screamed, but I couldn't get straight. I couldn't regain my balance.

My feet slipped.

I was falling.

CHAPTER 14

As I SLID sideways off the log, my balance shot, I pushed off with everything I had, the spikes below swimming in my panicked vision. Shields falling away, I reached out, stretching to grab the platform on the other side holding the gold. My palm hit the edge. I clutched it in a death grip, the weight of my body trying to rip my fingers away, and then grasped it desperately with my other hand.

An arrow now and I'd be done. But no arrow drove into my flank. No spear struck my back.

Gritting my teeth, I pulled myself up by my fingertips. Chin above the platform, I threw my arms over the edge one at a time. Body shaking, various points throbbing in agony, I pulled up a knee. Slowly but surely, I rolled myself onto the platform.

Only my rapid breathing and the thrumming of my heart in my ears interrupted the vast silence.

"Am I dead?" I asked myself, closing my eyes for a brief moment. That had to be the mantra of these trials, and now I'd taken it up. *Am I dead?* I almost laughed. Almost. There was no point in scrambling for cover. If Mr. Sunshine had wanted to kill me, he'd had his opening.

Pete's voice drifted across the space. "I literally *cannot* believe it. Do you see? Didn't I tell you he was good? He's so dang good! This is why the Sandman showed an interest. See?"

Pete clearly had low expectations. I was bleeding from multiple places, dog tired, and I'd nearly fallen to my death. This, when I'd had a team of people to help me. I wasn't expecting an award for brilliance, that was for sure. Still, I had made it. That counted for something. And we were one step closer to the gold.

I slowly rolled onto my stomach and shoved onto my hands and knees.

The spear thrower stood without a spear in hand, watching me. On the other side, I barely made out Mr. Sunshine (I still couldn't bring myself to call him what everyone else did) sitting in his chair, just watching. This leg of the challenge was complete.

I really hoped I hadn't just gotten through the easy part, but I had a feeling that might very well be the case.

Ethan stood at the beginning of the log, his expression curious, his body poised and ready. He didn't intend to let me take that gold without him. The others fanned out around him, grinning at me. Wally put up a thumb, smiling wide.

"Next," I said softly, no longer excited for the challenge to come. No longer feeling the confidence in the pit of my stomach. The struggle to survive the log challenge had exhausted me.

The sliding glass door slid open before me, and I crossed the threshold into the circular white room beyond. The gleaming floor squeaked under my soles. The mountain of gold glittered in the harsh light—and so did the metal weapons of all shapes and sizes that hung on hooks and rested on cloth-covered tables throughout the room.

Another step inside and it was like someone had flicked a switch. The feeling went from stagnant to expectant.

I cupped my knee, applying a little pressure to the throbbing wound before rubbing the back of my neck. My fingers came away red. Super, I was in tiptop shape for some sort of weapon-loving nutcase to come at me for dirtying their white room. At least, I figured that's what was about to happen.

But as I stood there, the pregnant pause intensified. The pressure increased. Danger lurked, waiting for its moment to attack. The feeling of dread from earlier strengthened, overwhelming and suffocating.

"Come at me then," I said softly, taking a step closer to the gold. "You're there, somewhere. I know it, you know it, and you know I know it. So *come at me*."

One more step toward the gold. That would be the trigger, I knew, but then what? Where would the jack jump out and with what weapon?

My knife hung heavy at my side, a dwarf compared to some of those hanging on the wall. I took another step. Then another—ten feet away now, and I could barely breathe over the tension. One more step and a scraping sound from behind me rang out in the silence.

Instead of spinning around and showing my back to the closed inner door, a potentially lethal mistake, I stepped diagonally and cocked my head, using peripheral vision. The door I'd come through slid shut and a sheen—a see-through wall—dropped down from the sky, trapping me in. My watch vibrated against my wrist. I'd expected no less. What I didn't understand, however, was where the sound had come from.

The gold shimmered, twinkling even without extra light from outside, before blinking out. Another illusion. There wasn't a single coin left.

"Nice," I said sarcastically, backing up to the side of the glass door, my back to a solid wall.

I touched it to be sure.

The door behind the fake pile of gold slid open, revealing a slender woman with blonde hair, most recently seen cutting the rope while Pete was climbing up. I'd assumed she was with the other girls.

I stopped myself from saying, "*You!*"

She grinned as though she guessed at my restraint. Then she winked at me, mischievousness twinkling in her eyes.

"Welcome to the Culling Trials," she said in a mid-range voice with no defining characteristics. "I am a sophomore student in the House of Shade. One year ago, I beat this trial and claimed the gold. This year, I was hand selected to usher the new students in should any actually make it this far."

"And kill them where appropriate?"

She smiled. "Maim only, of course." She stepped forward and the door slid shut behind her.

"So how does this work?" I asked, feeling a strange tingle through my body. "You try to maim me, and I try to…what? Maim you?"

Her smile increased in wattage. "Take me down, of course. If you can get me to yield, you can have the gold. Fail, and you will go to the healers."

Healers. That was good news.

A throwing star sailed toward my face. I hadn't even seen her move!

"Holy—" I just barely dove out of the way, rolling

across the white floor. Another sawed the air after me, tugging at my shirt as it zipped by. Best to keep moving.

I scrambled up as a third throwing star skittered against the ground where I'd just been. The woman had great aim, but she was slow at anticipating my movements. I had to use that to my advantage.

Similar weapons littered the table two feet away. I snatched up a throwing star, larger and with more prongs than the ones she was using, twisted and threw. I expected a wobbling mess that would buy me only a little time. Instead, the weapon flew fast and true, spinning through the air perfectly, directly toward her stomach.

Her eyes widened minutely, and she dodged out of the way, her fluid movements speaking of natural skill honed with training. I grabbed a mace from a nearby shelf, having absolutely no intention of getting closer to her and swinging the thing. No, I just threw it, my aim good and my expectations low.

She pivoted and dodged, easily evading, before dodging again, this time barely getting out of the way of a really neat ax that would've struck her with its handle. I wasn't an experienced ax thrower.

"You are a mess," she said, grabbing an army knife with a wicked serrated edge from the nearest table.

"That's Hot Mess to you, sweet cheeks." I snatched up a whip, wanting something long that could keep her at a distance. I needed a plan of attack, and until I had it, I intended to stall. As tired as I was, I was used to long, hard days. I would have bet my last dollar she'd never wrestled a cow in her life, let alone a bull the size of Whiskers for hours on end.

She ran forward, her knife held by the hilt, the business end pointed to the side. It was clear she knew how to use the thing.

I flicked the whip, once again not expecting much. The tip flew out and snapped viciously, right next to her head. The sound reverberated through the room.

Her eyes widened again, larger this time, and she changed direction, heading for the other side. Behind her, through the sheen of hardened air, I caught a glimpse of Ethan in the middle of the log, the end of his wand glowing as arrows bounced off of some sort of magical shield. That sure would've been helpful to me. Wally stood behind him and Gregory behind her. In front of all of them, keeping Ethan put despite his magic, was what looked like a badger.

Where the hell had the badger come from?

A knife flew out of nowhere, dragging my focus back into the room. I jerked to the right and it flew past my head. I flicked the whip again, the handle strangely comfortable in my grip, like shaking hands with a long-lost friend. It cracked against her forearm, opening a three-inch-long gash.

"How did someone so young master such a weapon?" she asked, frustration ringing in her voice.

I had no idea, so I just grinned at her. "Natural talent."

Her left hand zipped past her hip and a knife blossomed out of nowhere. It turned through the air, end over end, passing my face in crystal clarity.

I snapped the whip. The end slashed across her upper arm, slicing through fabric and skin. Blood welled up.

She dove, tucking into a somersault at the last minute. I readied the whip, but she was too quick, already inside my strike zone. I threw the whole thing at her and picked up a dagger with a long blade.

She popped up like she was on springs. Her fist, lightning fast, connected with my nose. My head snapped back and my eyes watered. I dodged a hook, staggering out of the way.

Terrible idea.

In a fluid movement, she swung her foot around, striking my chest. The breath left my lungs and I flew backward, knocked into a table full of weapons and dragged the whole lot down on top of me. A blade cut my arm and a knife point jabbed my leg. Pain screamed through me as I climbed to my feet.

She danced toward me, lovely and graceful, horribly

lethal. Her knife slashed the air.

I stopped improvising. Time to use what I knew.

I ripped my knife from my hip, comfortable and familiar in a way none of these other weapons could be. I dodged her knife thrust and countered with one of my own, raking the short but sharp blade across her skin.

She sucked in a breath and tried to pivot, but I was on her, jabbing, not worried about doing her harm. I was sure a healer could take care of her as easily as he or she could me.

She dove, rolled, bounced up, and a throwing knife sailed through the air. I smacked it away, hitting the handle and shocking the hell out of myself. I hadn't meant to do that, hadn't even thought it was possible!

She stepped closer, struck at me with her knife, missed, and punched me in the face. Blood leaked down my mouth and my eye started to swell, but I didn't stop. Couldn't. I'd come too far to get knocked down in the final hour.

I pushed forward, topping her by six inches and having a much longer reach. I jabbed her side with my knife, ignoring the part of my mind that quailed at assaulting someone with a deadly weapon. If I'd learned anything, it was that there would be no jail time here. No repercussions.

She let out a pain-filled grunt but didn't slow.

I dodged her strike, staying outside of her arm span, before striking again. She blocked and sliced across my arm. Pain bit deep with jagged claws, weakening my knees, but I blocked it out and slid my blade home, punching a hole in her other side. She staggered like a drunk, holding one arm tightly with the other.

Seizing my advantage, and putting my long legs to good use, I kicked out at her shin, missed, stepped back, and raked my other leg across her thigh. Her legs flew out from under her, taking her to the ground.

Snarling and shouts filled the room. Light blared.

Ethan.

Throwing knives flew from god knew where, one sinking into his leg.

Acting fast, I bent to finish the job, clunking the handle of my knife against the woman's forehead. Her lights went out, and she went limp. The headache when she awoke would be immense, and that was strangely satisfying.

When I sat back, panting, multiple places aching or on fire with pain, Ethan shot a jet of light at the woman's chest as she lay there. Her body shook with whatever he'd done.

"No," I said, waving him away. "I already did it. I—"

The gold shimmered back into the room, as solid as when I'd first seen it. The door at the back slid open and colored lights glowed down from the ceiling. Grinning faces filed in even as the badger took up a post in front of the gold, snarling at a red-faced Ethan.

"You did it," a dark-skinned man said with a gleaming, white-toothed smile, clapping as he positioned himself next to the table of gold. "I think this might be the first time someone other than the House of Shade passed the final challenge in this trial."

"Wild did it," Wally said in frustration, her fists balled up. "Billy, I mean. Billy did it, and he didn't need to cheat."

"Will someone get that badger out of here?" the man said, not hearing Wally.

"*I* did it," I said, rising from the ground. Blood dripped from my chin. "I was the one that knocked her out."

The man paused, his smile slipping. His gaze roamed my various wounds.

Ethan laughed to cover the moment. "You fought the good fight, surely," he said, all ease and confidence. His charisma filled the room and then some, ever the handsome trust fund baby who would rule the world one day. "But we both know it was my spell work that actually took her out. Look at you. You wouldn't have lasted much longer. If I hadn't finished her off, we'd have lost."

"He shouldn't know those spells." Wally flung a finger at Ethan. "Someone prepared him for this course. That's against the rules! His spell work is too advanced for someone his age."

"There's no rule against spell work once you're in the trials," Ethan said with a million-dollar smile, walking over to shake hands with the dark-skinned man. "I'm ahead of my class. What can I say?"

The man's brow furrowed. "It does seem that there was more than one player in this challenge. That is a first, too, I believe."

"Ethan just waited until Wild did all the hard stuff," Gregory said from the corner. "He didn't do anything. Billy, I mean."

If the man's eyebrows lowered any more, they'd become a mustache. "You're…Billy?" he asked me.

I realized with a start that somewhere along the way, I'd lost my hat. I plucked at my shirt to make sure no breast definition showed, then smoothed my hair back. Blood continued to drip from my nose and I pinched it shut, half to hide my face.

Maybe I *should* give Ethan the limelight. I couldn't have the scrutiny. I didn't need anyone realizing I wasn't who I claimed to be.

I shrugged. "Ethan did make his way in here," I finally said.

Wally sagged and the badger—Pete??—snarled louder

and kicked with his back feet, claws scratching across the floor. A distinct smell of rank musk floated off him. Gregory looked at the ground in the corner, his shoulders drooping.

I was letting my crew down by giving way to the rich, handsome kid that had it all, but I didn't have any choice. Not if I wanted to keep my anonymity. Stick to the middle, that's what I needed to do. My whole family's safety depended on it. And they meant more to me than any bunch of kids I'd only just met.

"Yes, well, we'll get it sorted out." The man smiled and gestured Ethan toward the door. "Come on, let's introduce you around. Or do you know everyone already?"

The two of them laughed, already as thick as thieves, leaving us all in their wake.

CHAPTER 15

THE WHITE ROOM slowly emptied of everyone but Wally, Pete—okay, assuming the badger was Pete—Gregory, and me, still kneeling in a growing puddle of blood. I'd never been so sore in my life, not even after Mr. Whiskers had first come home and run me over.

"Why would you let him take it?" Wally asked. "The officials would most likely believe you, you know. No one outside of the House of Shade ever gets the gold in this trial."

I tipped my head back and struggled to breathe around the blood sliding down my throat. "Some things aren't worth the fight. Gregory, explain to her why we never would have gotten that gold."

He snorted. "We are lesser than them, girl," he said, his tone bitter. "They would have found a reason to not believe us even if Ethan hadn't made it across. Had we all been from the House of Shade, sure, but with Ethan Helix here? Well, that gives them another thing to take from us. Another thing to lord over us."

I waved a hand in the air. "See?"

The badger let out a snarl, followed by a groan. I made myself watch as Pete shifted back to human right in front of me. His body kind of twisted in on itself, there was a moment where the air around him shimmered, and then it was just him on the floor.

Buck naked.

I jerked my head away. "Welcome back, Freckles. A badger, huh?"

"How could you do it, Wild? How could you let him win after everything? And I'm a honey badger." He stood and I closed my one eye that wasn't swelling shut.

"Because, she knows when to let them win, so that there can be a bigger pay off later. That is the proper way to play the long game," a new voice said softly, like a whispered hiss that crawled along my spine.

I spun on my knees, hands going for the weapons closest to me. There, standing just behind Wally, was a kid about our age, his skin so pale, it was near translucent in spots, showing the veins in his face and neck. Dressed all in black, he would have blended into the shadows easily.

"He," I snapped. "I'm a guy, goth boy. Who the hell are you and how did you get in here?"

His eyes fluttered to half-mast. "I am one of your crew. I followed you into the trial, though you did not see me, and followed the others on the log bridge to this place."

"Vampire," Pete said. "That's what he is. Creepy buggers. They might as well be in the House of Shade for how blinking sneaky they are. Sneaky sneakers!"

I kept my eyes on the—Jesus, vampires were real? I'd thought Gregory had been joking—new guy. There was an edge to him. Like one of the young bull calves at home who hadn't yet figured out they could be stronger than the rest of us. One day he'd be dangerous—deadly even. The possibility was there at least.

"What's your name?" I asked, pushing to my feet slowly, painfully.

"Orin," he said softly, his eyes dilating as he eyed me up. No, not me.

The blood dripping off me. His gaze tracked the drops as they fell and a pink blush covered his high cheekbones.

I arched an eyebrow with serious difficulty. "Come at me now, Orin, and we are going to have a seriously bad start to our relationship. I've had a crappy day, and you do not want to be the next person in line for a butt kicking."

I spat to the side for good, masculine effect, a gob of blood and saliva that hit with a thick thud. Vampires could smell really well, right? Was that why he'd called me 'she'? Could he know I was a girl? Morning crap on toast, I did not need him spilling the beans about my own little illusion.

"I can control the blood lust," he said, though the strain in his voice said otherwise. "I could not have come to the trials if I was not capable of that much. I would come with you, all of you. If your...crew...will have me as a companion."

"No," Pete said. "Not a good idea, Wild. In fact, a very bad idea."

I kept my good eye on Orin. "Why should we let you in?"

"Because I was following you all along and none of you noticed," he said. There was not an ounce of smugness to him. He was just stating facts.

So that's what I had been picking up in the tunnel.

"Not good enough," Gregory said. "We'll be housed together and—"

"I despise Ethan Helix," Orin said. "We went to school together. I know his style."

Silence hung for a single beat, then Pete and Gregory all but jumped on each other to speak first.

"He's in."

"Yup, let's take him."

Orin and I continued to eye each other up. He twitched under my gaze and shrunk a little inside his black clothes. "You don't like me."

"I don't know you enough to not like you," I said.

But if I kept him close, there was less chance he'd rat me out to the officials. You didn't rat out part of your team—that was how the guy code worked, even I knew that much.

He bobbed his head like a bird of prey and then wrapped his arms around his upper body. "Fair enough. I will be sure to prove my worth. To all of you."

Part of me wondered how he'd gotten to the top platform after the rope was cut. But if Pete was right, and Orin was a master of sneaking, he could have even taken a different path. Hell, he could have flown up here for all that I knew about vampires.

I sighed and turned as a new someone stepped into the doorway that led out of the white room.

"Excuse me, does anyone have need of a healer?" The newcomer was a stunningly handsome man in his early thirties. From the corner of my good eye, I watched with faint amusement as Wally swooned a little, her eyelashes fluttering. I couldn't blame her, not really. He was quite the package with jet black hair and deep, bottomless brown eyes. His frame was lean, cut hard, and he was one of the few people I'd seen so far who was taller than me. A smile crossed his perfect lips and two fangs peeked out on either side. I steeled myself to keep from stepping back.

Another vampire. Was it coincidence?

He had a pair of sweatpants in his hand and he tossed them at Pete, who grabbed them in mid-air and yanked them on. Apparently, he could move fast when motivated.

"I am Jared," the older vampire said. "Supervisor of the Culling Trials. I see you've got one of mine with you." He glanced at Orin. Tension rose between them, taut, and behind me, I could feel Orin cringe under his gaze. I stepped sideways, cutting him from view. Orin was with us now, and that meant nobody was picking on him, not while I was around.

"Yeah, about that healer? Think you can take me there? I got a scratch or two," I said.

Jared snorted. "You Shades are all the same. Tough as nails and about as smart. Follow me."

I didn't let myself react, which was surely what he wanted.

He didn't turn, didn't walk away. He was just there one second and gone the next. I blinked my one good eye through the smudge of blood. "Am I seeing things?"

"Full vampires are extremely fast," Gregory said and then shook his head. "I seriously cannot understand how you don't know anything about our world and still…" he waved his ridiculously skinny fingers back the way we'd come, "...have done all that. And won. Despite what Ethan said, we all know that you won this trial, Wild."

"Sheltered. *He* has been sheltered and that makes *his* fear less," Orin whisper-hissed. I turned to give him a glare. Yeah, he knew I was a girl.

I blinked and he was gone too. Just like that Jared dude. I narrowed my eyes until I could pick out the subtle outline of his head in the single solid shadow at the back of the room. "I can see you, Orin."

Hide and seek was going to get old fast, but I didn't have the energy to do anything about it at the moment. The cuts all over me throbbed, making themselves well known now that the adrenaline had faded. I blew out a breath, only able to breathe through my mouth. "Let's get out of here."

Wally stepped up beside me and tucked herself under my arm. "Lean on me. You know that sepsis can set in within hours of a cut and it causes thousands of deaths a year. That would go poorly on all of us."

Pete stepped up on the other side and I dropped an arm across his shoulders. "You're a real downer, Wally."

"I know," she said with a small smile. "It's what I do. You'll be glad for it one day though."

"Doubtful," Pete muttered.

Gregory rolled his eyes as he passed us and took the lead. I assumed Orin fell in behind us but didn't bother to check.

The hall that led out of the white room was serviceable solid concrete and blessedly short seeing as each step sent new shockwaves of pain up through my body until Wally and Pete were all but carrying me. I almost apologized to them. But that's something Wild the girl would do, not Wild the boy.

I clamped my jaw shut and just worked on breathing through the pain and not passing out. Head down, I put one foot in front of the other. Thank God this was over.

We stepped out of a final door and into the bright sunlight of a late summer day in upstate New York.

The sudden change in scenery threw me for a loop and I took a minute to breathe it all in, to taste it on the back of my tongue.

We were at the end of the trial. I'd made it.

A white tent with a red cross emblazoned on it was set up in the grass ahead of us. All of the flaps to the tents were pulled wide, allowing medical staff to easily go between them. A few of the guys from the Bro Pack were being treated by what looked like doctors. One of the guys had burns all over his hands, and I had no doubt he'd been caught by a blast of electricity while climbing the metal wall. The blonde chick I'd fought in the white room was there too, stretched out on her back on one of cots.

I did a slow turn of my head. This wasn't the only tent. There were more tents to either side of us, at what had to be the exits for the other trials, and each was overflowing with patients.

Crying, whimpering, yelps of pain echoed through the air.

"Is he missing an arm?" Wally asked.

"Holy cats." Pete gulped heavily, "that one's belly is sliced open."

"Keep walking," I said, and they stumbled forward, jarring me. For just a second, I thought I was going to vomit, the pain was so bad. Surely the cuts I'd gotten couldn't be this bad?

I swallowed the nausea down with difficulty and closed my eyes. Two sets of hands gripped me, pulling me forward the second my eyes drifted shut. I snapped an arm up, breaking away, and opened my good eye.

"Easy. We're going to help you out here. My name is Mara. I'll be your healer today." The voice was soft and soothing, and it belonged to a woman who looked equally soft. Her body was all curves and there would have been no hiding her as a boy at any point in her life. Her kind, gentle smile calmed me enough that I let her guide me to one of the beds. "You Shades, always so defensive."

There it was again. Shade. I'd been well and truly labelled. I doubted I'd even need the sticker name tag any longer.

I lay on the bed, unable to hold back a groan. I wanted to make a smartass comment, but I decided to leave that up to someone else for once.

The woman—Mara—put a hand on my forehead and then one on my belly. "Dirty tricks in this trial, the blades were edged with a nerve-damaging agent to make the pain worse. I bet you're feeling pretty low right now."

I opened my mouth to answer and ended up rolling to the side, puking into a bucket that had been strategically placed. I gagged and spat, my nose plugged with blood and my throat clogged with puke.

"Don't you worry. I'll get you all fixed up and then you can have your banquet." She leaned into me, her hands pressing hard against both head and belly.

I groaned, sucked in a slow breath, and my body heaved as if I were going to puke again.

"Hold on, this will be uncomfortable," Mara said with that gentle voice. My skin tingled under her touch, like her flesh was covered in tiny hot pokers that went from being warm and soothing to so hot they burned. But I held still, shaking so hard the table rattled and my feet banged against the foot of the gurney.

Wally and Pete were close to my head, and I focused on their voices as Mara did her thing.

"Wally," Pete whispered, "are they pulling a blanket

over that kid's head? Is he dead?"

"Yes, he is," she said. "I see his spirit leaving him. Sad, he fell and snapped his neck when he landed."

I shuddered and was going to open my eyes, but Mara slid her hand over them. "Let's get these fixed up for you. And that nose. It would be awful to have it set crooked."

"Why? Chicks dig scars," Pete said. "Let him keep his crooked nose."

Mara's hands tensed at that word—*him*.

Oh. She was a healer, trained in the human body, of course she would know I was a girl. Probably when her magic delved me, she could tell the difference. I was a fool. How was I going to keep this up?

I reached up and pulled her hands from my eyes. "Leave the nose."

I put all the pleading I could into my eyes, begging her not to give up my secret. She frowned, her cupid's bow mouth curving downward. "All right. For now, I'll heal it as it is. But if you change your mind, we can fix it later."

"Thanks."

"You might have residual pain through tomorrow, and your appetite will be huge, but don't overdo it in one go. Small meals, spaced out if you can. You'll be ready in no time for the next trial." Mara stepped back and I found myself staring at her, still flat on my back. Her words rang in my ears as though they'd been spoken in another language.

"How many of these trials are there again?" I asked with numb lips. "Also, can we skip any?"

Mara's eyes were a little amused. "Five. You've successfully made it through your first trial, plus the bonus. You're off to a great start. But you'll have to run all five, young…man. One for each house, to be sure you are placed right."

All…five.

My jaw dropped and I spluttered, at a loss for words. Or maybe not. "Are you yanking my chain?"

"Texan," Wally muttered.

Gregory cleared his throat. "We need to have a discussion, Wild. We are a crew now and—"

I waved my hands across my body, cutting him off. "Not here." I couldn't say why, but I wanted to keep my lack of knowledge as close to the chest as possible.

Before I could even leave the cot, my most favorite of favorite people arrived on scene.

Mr. Sunshine. Sideburns himself.

And he wasn't alone.

The world dropped away, dizzying, flipping everything inside me upside down. A rush of relief and comfort washed over me, bathing me.

I'm not alone.

A moment later, though, a newfound rage burned me through.

I stared, unable to believe who stood in front of me. Unable to believe that he had really come here, despite all we'd been through, and not said a word.

There, in the flesh, standing in front of me with a bloody blank face on his fool head was Rory Wilson.

I hadn't wanted to believe this moment would come. I hadn't wanted to believe my father. Rory should've had a better life in Nevada. He should've found a calm woman who never caused trouble and started a family.

Instead, he'd run full steam into more danger than he'd left.

He'd been here when my brother had died.

I could barely speak, I was so angry, and I completely ignored the traitorous memories of what he'd been to me. He'd been my protector when I'd been up to my eyeballs in bad decisions, my watchdog when I hadn't needed protecting, and my partner in crime when I'd wanted to have a little fun. He'd been part of my world.

But he'd lied. Pushed me away. Left a note and snuck off in the night like a coward.

He had let my brother die.

My childhood buddy and fellow heathen was my soon-to-be nemesis.

Chapter 16

I WAS UP and off the table in the medic tent in a flash, stomping my way across the small space between Rory and me. In those few seconds, I took him in, my first look after two years of nothing but memories.

He'd grown in the time we'd spent apart, muscling up, hardening into a man. Sure, he was still Rory, but…not. He no longer looked like the boy who'd left rural Texas for a better life. His hair was shorter, he had a new scar along the side of his jaw, and there was an aura of danger rolling around him.

Sideburns held up a hand. "I need to speak with you, *Billy*."

I smacked his hand out of the way and kept moving until I was nose to neck with Rory. "You have some nerve showing up here, Wilson. You couldn't be bothered to even come to Tommy's funeral. You lied about where you were going and now you show up with this cuntasaurus rex at your side? What the ever-living hell?"

His smell permeated my world, and my stomach fluttered. Clean cotton, spice, and a hint of vanilla. Home. He smelled like home, and good memories and nostalgia rolled me like a wave.

My mouth dropped open. I hadn't realized that smell was his until this moment. That smell had been there when I was at the airport getting mugged. "You helped them kidnap me, too, you sick sonuvabitch? Wow, you've sure changed. From a cool guy I used to know to a real sack of crap."

Pete groaned. "He's going to get us all killed."

"He's definitely getting closer to death, I'll give you that," Wally said quietly. "Be careful, Wild."

Rory jerked a little when Wally used my nickname. He stared down at me. "Nice to see you too Johnson. Your brother's death was a shame, but that's what you get when you aren't cut out for the academy. You die. You'd best remember that."

I sucked in a sharp breath, his words worse than any blow from any weapon. I snapped a fist out in a hard hook, directly into his left side, driving it as hard as I could. He bent at the waist as he took the blow, a whoosh of air escaping him. I stepped back and he slowly straightened, face pale. I tipped my chin up, anger making my traitorous eyeballs water.

Damn him, he could always bring out the worst in me as well as the best. I could feel the angry tears pooling in the corners of my eyes. Definitely not a manly trait to cry when you were angry. I sucked in a slow breath, pushing the emotions down. "You were always sloppy on the left. Nice to see *one* thing hasn't changed."

His face tightened, jaw clamped, and eyes narrowed.

Sideburns stepped between us. "Enough." His voice cracked through the air and more than a few people straightened as if he'd snapped them in the ass with a whip.

I turned my glare on him. "What? You going to try and knife me here, in front of everyone?"

He grabbed my arm and dragged me through the tent as though he were pulling a child along with him. "You will listen to me now, *Billy*, or you are going to get yourself killed." He took something from his back pocket—the hat I'd lost—and jammed it on my head with enough force to make me wince.

"Now you want to act like you're trying to help me? That's a pile of horse crap, and I know horse crap, Sunshine. I used to shovel it—"

He came to a dead stop. "What. Did. You. Call. Me?"

Oops.

I hadn't meant for that to slip out. "Sideburns," I quickly amended, followed by a pronounced wince. Worse still!

He pulled off his aviators and his eyes were as dangerous and dark as I'd imagined, darker because I could see death in the black pools. He was a killer through and through, of that there was zero doubt. "There are more forces at play here than you realize. At some point, it will make sense. But for now, keep your head down and your hands clean. Stay out of the limelight." I couldn't help but glare. Anger at Rory still coursed through me and made me stupidly bold. "You threatened my family, so I'm here. You know—"

He jerked me closer so we were nose to nose, forcing me to stoop just a little. Strangely, though, he seemed bigger even though I looked down on him. "I know what you are, *Billy*. Let's keep it to only me knowing. And stick to the middle ground, you idiot. You stand out, and what do you think is going to happen? People are going to notice you. You don't want that, not here."

There was an unspoken threat there. But I wasn't one for unspoken anything.

"Or what?"

His hand tightened on me. "You'll have to watch your siblings come through the trials and see them die firsthand. You might survive here, but do you think they will?" he growled. "Right now, you being here can protect them. Just like you wanted. But only if you keep the illusion up as long as possible."

He let me go, shoving me a little so I stumbled back.

"I've got my eye on you, *Billy*. Don't fuck up."

With a snap of his fingers, he turned to leave. Rory studied me for a silent beat before turning without a word and following his new bestie. But I'd seen the flash of mirth in his eyes. The twinkle of excitement. That look had always meant we were about to get into something incredibly foolhardy and dangerous. I hardly knew the guy I'd grown up with anymore while still knowing him like the back of my hand.

First, he'd lied to me, then dismissed my brother's death, and now he was helping Sideburns?

Fire burned through me even as my heart cracked.

I gritted my teeth to prevent myself from going after him. He'd get his; I'd make sure of it. But right now, I had to look after me. Me and my new crew. He wasn't the only one with a new bunch around him.

I slapped away a trail of hot tears down my face. They had no place in this setting, especially with the image I needed to maintain.

I fisted my hands at my sides and turned away from them to see Gregory, Pete, Wally and Orin watching me with wide eyes.

"Did you…talk back to the Sandman?" Pete whispered. "You've got to have the biggest balls of any guy I know! You're my freaking hero!" He clapped a hand on my back and tried to get me in a half hug, which I slid out of. Just in case.

"I hope you live long enough for the next trial," Wally said, all seriousness.

Orin snorted and covered his lips with a hand. I glared at him until he withered under my gaze. Look at me making friends wherever I went.

"Where do we go from here?" I asked. I needed to change the subject. I needed to protect Sam and Billy with everything I had and that meant pulling my crap together.

"You follow me. As it should be."

The five of us turned to see the blond pretty boy, Ethan, standing there, his wand tucked through a loop on his belt, hands on his hips. Like a wannabe Peter Pan if I ever saw one.

"We aren't going anywhere with you," Pete snapped.

I nodded. "What he said." Tipping my head, I added, "And where's your Tinker Bell?"

Ethan glared at me, his face going slightly pink. "Just what are you implying?"

"That you look like Peter Pan, idiot," Gregory said. "The stupidity of the House of Wonder truly mystifies me. How in the world you got to the top of the food chain is beyond my ken."

I pointed at the goblin. "What he said."

"You don't have a choice," Ethan said, ignoring us.

"We finished our first trial together, which means we are a unit in each subsequent trial whether any of us like it or not. Assuming you all survive, that is."

He walked toward me, bumping me with his shoulder as he went by. Or trying to. I didn't so much as budge an inch and I watched with amusement as he lifted a hand to rub his own shoulder. "They are announcing the winners of today's trials. Then we eat and get tomorrow off."

I didn't want to follow Ethan, but…I needed to keep a low profile, and Peter Pan would clearly steal any spotlight he caught a glimmer of. Maybe staying around him wasn't such a bad idea.

I glanced at my…friends? Were they friends? Yeah, they were. "Come on, we're with stupid."

Pete's face said it all, he did not want to do this. And I didn't blame him. "Seriously? After the stunt he pulled?"

I shrugged. "If he dies in the next round, we're done with him. That's got to give you hope."

Wally hurried up next to me. "Depending on the trial we face, that is highly plausible. Though, with him being a Helix, I suppose those numbers drop. Likely he will have some superior training to help him survive." Her lips pursed and I could almost see her working the odds out in her head.

The group of us followed Ethan like a flock of sheep to a shepherd. He never once looked back, as though he was so sure we'd follow.

Lambs to the slaughter.

"Let's see how we can make it work to our advantage," I said to the others in an undertone. "If he has knowledge about what's coming, then all the better."

Gregory was the first to nod his agreement. "We will all be more likely to survive with him in our group, that is true. Being a Helix will give him special privileges."

They were quiet a moment, and surprisingly it was Orin who spoke next. "I'll keep an eye on him. Like I mentioned, I know his style. He'll play us like a fiddle if we let him."

Gregory waved a hand. "No need. We will be dorming together. With the exception of our necromancer. No girls allowed. She might peek at us in the shower."

Necromancer. I whipped my head around to stare at Wally, remembering the comment before the trial about walking memory banks. It made more sense now. But her name tag didn't have a designation under it like mine did. Like Gregory's did. Pete's had fallen off, but there was no doubt about Orin. "You can raise the dead?"

She shrugged. "Maybe. I won't know until all my training is done. But my chance of ending up in the House of Night is close to ninety-nine percent seeing as my entire family has trained there on both sides, going back four generations."

And then the rest of what Gregory had said slipped into my brain. "Wait, we'll *dorm* together?"

"Yes, the five guys will dorm together. And Wally will be put into the girls' dorm. Maybe in another group." Gregory rubbed at his pointed nose. "I smell roast beef."

"I smell it too," Pete said, grabbing at his flabby stomach as it let out a loud growl.

With the guys following their noses—and Ethan—I let myself drop back a few steps.

Orin fell in beside me. He said nothing for a moment and then spoke quietly. "I won't tell."

"Why?"

The question I asked was just as quiet, Sideburns's warning still ringing through me. "You don't even know me."

He tucked his hands into the bottoms of his long sleeves so they disappeared. "You drew me to this group…my mother was a seer and I have a little of her talent. I need to be here, with you and the others. Besides, you let me into this group without much hesitation. Which, considering what I am, is saying something."

I frowned. "Somehow a vampire is worse than a goblin?"

His lips twitched upward. "Depends on who you ask. But most would not sleep in a dorm with a vampire. I don't believe that Ethan even realizes I am part of this group. He won't like it when he does."

"That's going to matter why?" I frowned as I worked through everything he was saying. He thought he was meant to be here, which was fine—weird, but fine—but he also thought I'd drawn him to the group. I'd done nothing but do my thing. Run across a log. Beat up a girl. Dodge electricity. Outpace some golems.

Right?

"It's going to matter because he is terrified of vampires." Orin grinned then, showing off the tiniest set of fangs I'd ever seen. Smaller than the barn cats at home.

"I've seen housecats with bigger teeth," I muttered.

His grin slid. "They get bigger when I am inducted as a full vampire."

"I bet all the guys say that."

Orin laughed. "Your secret is safe with me. Be careful though. I do not know if the others would feel the same way. And there is a chance they'll be able to figure it out. If Pete figures out his sniffer. If Gregory looks too close."

I nodded, not because I didn't trust the others but because it seemed like the thing to do. I would do the best I could with what I had, and hope it was enough.

We followed Ethan across an open field and up a slight incline. At the top of the slope, the view spread in front of us like a scene straight out of a fairy tale. A mansion sprawled in the shallow of the valley below. Five floors of brick and ivy and dormer windows. The grounds were immaculate and movement drew my eye to the side. A caretaker walked with a pair of shears, cutting and trimming, his back bent, movements slow.

Pete, Wally, Gregory, and even Orin gasped a little and excitement bubbled out of them. "The mansion is bigger than I expected!"

"It's every bit as plush; you can tell from here."

"Brilliant!"

Call me a pessimist, but with my luck and the Grim Reaper aka Sideburns as my guardian angel, there wasn't a hope in hell we'd be staying in luxury. "Don't get your hopes up. The job here is to break us, I think. Giving us a cushy mansion dorm would not fit with that," I said.

Ethan snorted and smirked. "Please. I'm a Helix. We'll have the best rooms. You can thank me later."

I wanted to bet him that he was wrong. But I had nothing to bet but…the money in my backpack that awaited me when I left the medical tent. A flush of excitement cut through the worry.

I held out a hand. "What do you want to bet we get shoved into a grimy little nothing of a hole?"

A slow grin spread across his face. "How about a portion of that gold *I won* back there?"

Pete was all but vibrating, but he held it together.

Kind of. "You're a nasty piece of work, aren't you? Slimy House of Wonder crap."

I nodded but kept my eyes on Ethan. "And if I lose, I'll give you the cash I have in my backpack."

I thought he'd tell me I'd have to leave the trials. It's what I would have asked from him.

His grin widened. "Done."

I turned my palm up and he slapped his hand into it. A burst of sparkles erupted from the connection that seemed to surprise even Ethan, though he covered it up quickly.

I pulled my hand back and waved him forward. "Lead on, mighty Helix. Let's see where you can take us." I already knew though, and if Ethan was going to be dumb as a post, I'd happily take his gold. Seeing as it was really my gold in the first place, I didn't feel bad, not one bit.

He strode forward down the hill, arms swinging like he was the king of the world.

And maybe he was with all his magic and money. But that didn't mean I couldn't take him down a peg or two. I grinned as I watched him stride away.

Maybe this would be a little fun after all.

CHAPTER 17

"BUT *HOW* DID you know?" Gregory insisted as we stepped up to the rundown portable housing off to the side of the mansion. The siding had come off in places and the screens on the windows had been torn away from the inside going out, which was less than comforting. The stairs leading up to the one door were barely twelve inches across and looked to be held up by chunks of rotting wood.

I'd won the bet, sure, but we were the losers no matter how you looked at it.

The best part of the whole situation? Not all the teams got shafted. Some of them did end up in the mansion in the lap of luxury, but not us. And that had chafed Ethan's chaps like nothing else could have. All his friends got to stay in the mansion.

He was the only kid from the House of Wonder who had been shoved out here with the riffraff in one of the rundown portables. That was enough to make me grin.

Gregory danced in front of me, barely dodging my

feet as I strode along. "How could you have possibly guessed? Even the necromancer thought there was no way you'd win that bet against a Helix."

Speaking of…Ethan was way behind us, still arguing with one of the school officials—one who happened to be his father. I slowed enough that I could overhear them.

"Why you would bet any of your portion of the gold is beyond me. Especially up against a Shade—you know how devious they are." Mr. Helix sighed heavily. "You can never trust the other houses, Ethan. This is a lesson for you, frustrating as it may be. One that would have come at some point or another."

I fought the urge to turn around and glare at the older Helix. Instead I spoke just loud enough that everyone could hear me. "Mr. Helix says we each get a cut of the gold. Ethan was wrong about taking it all. How magnanimous of him." There, let them chew on that big word.

Pete and Gregory did a fist bump, and Pete tried to follow it up with a chest bump that ended with him banging into Gregory in a rather awkward way. Gregory shook his head. "Beast shifters, seriously."

Orin pushed the door open and we all stared into the space that would be our home for however long we lasted here. Three sets of bunkbeds stared back at us. Nothing fancy, they could have been pulled out of the barracks of any army. Thin blankets, thinner pillows, and bedsprings that looked like they'd been completely stretched out.

It was the table of food laid out in between them that had my attention.

"Oh. My. Holy. Cats." Pete breathed out. "I *knew* I could smell roast beef."

He shoved past us as a tingle of warning slid down my spine. I hurried after him as he stared down at the food, literally drooling. His hand shot out, faster than I'd ever seen him move, and he had a handful of roast beef lifting to his mouth when I smacked it down.

"What the hell, Wild?" He stared up at me like I'd just told him Santa wasn't real. "I'm starving!"

"Just…wait a second." I frowned at the food as if glaring at it could make it give up its secrets. The enticing smells warred with the tingle of warning that still ran up and down my back. How many times had I kept Rory and my brother from eating the wrong mushrooms?

Ethan shoved between us. "It's a *banquet*, Johnson. I don't suppose you, in your piss-poor hovel of a town, would have ever been to one. But this is it. Copious amounts of food that has been cooked to be eaten."

He grabbed a tart and brought it to his mouth. I could have let him eat it.

But I wasn't sure it wouldn't kill him. I snapped a fist out and knocked it out of his hands.

"Something's wrong with it," I said. "Poison maybe."

My explanation seemed to have come a smidge too late. Ethan jumped at me, his hand going for his wand. I sidestepped and stuck a foot out, tripping him easily. He might have magic on his side, but he was no fighter. He crashed to the floor, where he immediately turned toward me and pointed his wand at my head. "There is nothing wrong with it. You stupid, vile, ignorant—"

"Umm, guys?" Pete waved a hand between us. "Some of the food is burning through the table."

We all whipped around to see the center section of tarts *melting* the plate and table below them. I backed up. "See? No *bueno*. No damn *bueno*."

"See, he's amazing! Wild knew. He knew this would kill us. Holy cats, you saved me. And…" Pete grimaced. "You saved Ethan? Why in the world would you do that?"

I didn't look at Ethan. "What does it matter? He's on our team. I don't have to like him to know that we have to work together to get through this." I stared at the food, stomach rumbling. Pete wasn't the only one starving.

Orin whispered from the shadows in the corner of the room. "You think they'll bring us more food? I'm getting awfully hungry."

"Shut up, vampire!" Ethan shouted, and for just a second, I thought I saw a glimmer of tears in those baby blues. Fear. He really was afraid of the vampire.

I frowned. "What are you so worked up about anyway? We aren't going to starve."

"This isn't how it's supposed to be! I am a Helix!" he roared, and with that he stomped out of the portable, slamming the rickety door behind him.

"Think he's going to get help?" Pete asked.

I nodded. "And complain. And somehow make it like we're to blame and he's the hero."

Gregory laughed, though it was a bitter laugh. "So, the usual?"

I gave him a half grin and nodded. "Yeah, the usual."

Using a couple of folding chairs as scrapers and a blanket as a catch all, we managed to get the food out of the portable and off to the side, away from our rickety stairs. The tarts were still smoking and something else was glowing a pale green in the dusky night.

"What if it was just the tarts that were bad?" Pete moaned, his stomach echoing him.

"You want to take that chance?" I asked.

He sighed. "No. But I'm *starving*. I'm going to fade away to nothing."

I tapped my fingers on my chin, thinking. "This was a final challenge for us, because of the trial we went through, right?" I looked to Gregory.

The small goblin nodded. "It would seem that way. Poison is one of the assassin's deadliest tools."

"Right, so here's the plan." I drew them in close and

gave them the rundown quickly, simply. The teams who'd gone through trials for the other houses would not have poison in their food, but they also likely wouldn't share. Which meant we were going to have to work for our supper.

The next closest portable was nearly pushed against us, but no way were we robbing our neighbors. No, we needed to venture further out and put enough portables between our target and us that they couldn't know who the culprit was.

"Orin, you think that you can take the lights out?" I directed as we jogged behind the row of portables.

"Yes, I'm adept at killing light sources." He jogged too, but made it look like floating, which was both creepy and cool.

"Pete?"

"Yup, I've got them." He held up two pillow cases, tossing one to me, and one to Gregory. As if we were going trick or treating. Only we weren't going to ask nicely for the food. More of a trick than a treat for those in the portable.

Gregory shook his head as he caught the pillow case. "This place is not supposed to be fun. Why does this feel like fun?"

I grinned at him.

Pete pointed a finger. "It's his fault. I don't know

how, but I know it's because of Wild."

Gregory didn't want to like me. I'd known that from the first moment I'd picked him up off that alley floor. He didn't want to like anyone. I'd known people like him growing up—the world treated them like dirt and they responded as though they didn't care. Rory had been like that when we'd first met.

Gregory didn't want to trust me, but I was winning him over.

I shrugged. "I'm hungry. You guys are hungry. What else is there? Let's get some grub."

God, I sounded like Rory in that moment. He'd said something like that to me to convince me to steal from the general store. I'd been caught with a bunch of bananas in my shirt. Rory had escaped unscathed as usual.

The four of us took up our positions. We'd start by knocking the lights out. Orin was on the roof and pulled the lines, a pop of wires letting go the only sound.

The portable went dark and a volley of shouts went up inside.

Next came Pete's job. He shifted into his honey badger shape and went crazy digging at the base of the portable, snarling and freaking out the entire time, his claws louder against the wood and metal than I would have thought possible. He sounded like a monster, and his efforts shook the portable. Gregory and I leaned in on the other side, shoving the building on its foundation. I glanced over to see him grinning from ear to ear. And I do mean ear to ear.

"Fun, right?" I whispered.

He snickered. "Way too much fun."

The shouting inside intensified and from the rooftop came a loud snarl and the sound of tin being ripped off. Orin was adding a nice touch.

A split second later, the door busted open and the guys from inside piled out on top of one another, racing straight for the mansion without looking back.

"Hurry! They won't take long to bring an official back," I picked up the pillow case and ran for the door. Orin re-attached the wiring and the lights popped back on in a blinding flash. I held up my hand a moment and then took a look at the food. They'd barely touched it.

Better than that, there was no warning tingle. No intuition that the food was off.

"It's good," I said, and we started stacking containers in the pillow cases. Under a minute and we had them both full and were making our way out of the portable.

"Hurry, they're coming back and they've got help!" Orin whisper-hissed as he dropped down from the roof. We bolted, heading toward the tree line that wrapped around the sides of the mansion. It would take us longer to get back to our own portable, but we'd have a better chance of keeping our food.

Pete caught up, still on four legs, still snarling and snapping. Gregory pulled a tart out and tossed it to him. "Shut your trap, Pete."

Pete. The first time he'd used his name. Maybe I wasn't the only one winning the goblin over.

We crouched in the shadows and watched as the five members of the group led someone toward the portable we'd just abandoned, and the official that followed was… "Oh, crap, that's—"

"The Sandman," Orin said ominously.

At least he wasn't wearing his sunglasses at night. That would have just made me ridicule him harder.

He took a quick look at the portable. "The lights are on."

"No, you don't understand, we were under attack!" one of the guys said, his voice so high-pitched he could have fit into the girls' dorms.

"Yeah, it was bad. Stuff was breaking, the lights went out, and I swear one of the beasts followed us out of the trial. I could hear it."

I held out a fist and Pete shifted to two legs and fist bumped me back. Score for our team.

The group circled away from us to look at the far side of the portable, and I tipped my head. "Let's go."

We hurried along the edge of the trees, and only once

did I look back, a tingle along my spine tipping me off. Sideburns stood outside of their portable, staring into the trees. His eyes swept over us, but they didn't slow. But he knew. I don't know how I knew, but I knew that he knew it was me.

I shuddered and hurried the guys along. Promises of food and a warm bed were all it took to make my feet move…until I remembered that I was covered in my own blood, sweat, and filth and could smell myself a mile off.

How was I going to shower with a room full of guys and not get caught?

CHAPTER 18

THE FOOD WAS gone faster than I'd thought possible, despite the healer's warnings not to eat too fast. But that brought me to my more pressing issue of just how to get clean when I was sharing such a small space with four guys. "Who wants first shower?" I asked, noticing the large trunks to either side of each set of bunk beds.

"You can go, if you want," Pete said, rolling into one of the bottom bunks. After his bellyaching about heights, it wasn't a surprising choice.

"Nah." I knelt beside one of the trunks, slipped the open padlock out of the metal hook, and flipped up the clasp. "I need a minute to let my food settle. You can go."

"I'm first." Ethan pushed open a trunk on the other side of the room before extracting plain gray sweats and a plain white T-shirt.

"Of course, you are," Pete mumbled as Gregory and Orin checked the trunks near their chosen beds.

What had just become my trunk held the same items as Ethan's, and shockingly, the pants went all the way to my ankles even though I was the tallest in the room. Had I gotten lucky with my trunk choice, or did these sweats somehow alter to fit the wearer? More magic, that was the only answer.

A feeling of vertigo washed over me. I braced against the wall. "This magic stuff is blowing my mind," I said as Ethan pulled off his shirt, revealing a toned chest that under other circumstances would have had me staring. "Magic is supposed to be made up. It isn't supposed to be real. Vampires, goblins, shifters, *wands...*" I rubbed my temples. "This can't be real life."

Ethan stalled at the bathroom door. "Looks like a communal shower." He turned back with a hard stare. "Four shower heads does not mean four people need to be crowding in. I don't need your hairy asses that close."

Pete groaned. "Could this place get any worse?"

"At least there's a door on the toilet," Orin said, peering in behind Ethan.

Ethan rolled his shoulders and flared his elbows. "Dude. Back your creepiness off."

Orin's blank stare took Ethan's measure before he slowly took one step back. "I wax."

"That's—" Ethan blew out a breath through his nose and shook his head, confusion and disgust radiating from him.

"What the hell have I gotten stuck with..." He continued into the bathroom.

"Don't your parents have magic? I mean, I assume one of them is a Shade," Pete asked me, scooting to the edge of his mattress so he could see me.

I pulled out a shirt and a pair of tighty-whities. "I honestly have no idea." I draped them over the bar of the bunk above Pete. Orin slipped into the bathroom. "But now that I'm here, some of the things my mother said throughout my childhood make me think she knew about all this. She must've, right?"

"Unless her parents excused her from the academy for some reason," Pete said. A squeak preceded the sound of running water from the bathroom. He must've read the confusion in my expression. "You can request to be pardoned from the Culling Trials, which then means you don't go to the academy. You'd go to normal school and live your life like someone without magic." He shivered. "I have no idea why someone would want that for their kid. It's no life, not when you could have this."

I snorted. This. Like the Culling Trials were some great opportunity?

Like the academy where Tommy had died was an even better place to be?

I fingered the hem of my sweats, my mind whirling. That was the life we'd lived on the farm. No magic. No talk of magic. Why would my parents willingly choose that for themselves and their kids if it was *lesser* in the magical society's mindset? Why would they hide all of this from us? It didn't make sense. I was missing something, I had to be.

I hated that she had to give it up because of a rumor about that curse.

My father had said that, muttered to himself after too much moonshine.

"What about your dad?" Gregory asked, cutting through my thoughts.

I shook my head slowly as Ethan's voice drifted out of the bathroom. "Dude, back off. I'm not going to tell you again." Apparently, Orin was taking his Ethan watching to a higher level.

"Dad never said anything. Until Sideburns showed up, he never once mentioned magic to me. But..." I thought back to what he'd said about Tommy coming here. About wanting to live through his son. I shook my head again. I didn't want to admit that he'd been a null. I didn't want the chance that they'd turn their noses up at my dad.

"Maybe they got kicked out of the Culling Trials," Gregory said as the water in the bathroom turned off.

I just grunted, thinking about what my dad had said. Wondering if it was true. Had my mom known Tommy's life would be in more jeopardy than the other students?

"That's why they have people like the Sandman," Pete said. "Well…not him specifically, but people that visit the worried parents. The recruiters almost always talk the parents around. It's really not *that* dangerous here."

"Dude. People *died* today," I said as Ethan emerged from the bathroom with a towel wrapped around his hips. Steam billowed around him and I had to rip my eyes away from the droplets of water clinging to his muscular chest. Yup, not looking, not looking at all.

"Yeah, but that hardly ever happens." Pete shrugged.

"Wild is right," Ethan said at his trunk. He pulled off his towel and I jumped, jerking my gaze to the metal bed frame in front of my face. Things were getting awkward. "Today's challenges had a record high death rate. Someone is going to get fired for that. I can guarantee it."

Pete rolled out of his bed and grabbed some sweats before hugging them to his chest and heading for the bathroom. Hopefully that meant stripping down in front of everyone and drying your balls wasn't common practice among men bunking together. At least not for everyone. Thank God, since I had no balls to dry.

"You coming?" Pete asked.

I jerked my head at Gregory, who was staring at me. "You go. I want to look and see if there are any boxers in here. I'd rather…freeball it."

"Spoken like a guy who's never played any sports,"

Ethan said, stepping into his underwear.

Now would've been a great time to take up smoking and excuse myself outside.

"What's next for tomorrow?" I asked, digging through my trunk to keep from peeking at a truly well-formed rear end. Not that I should know that about him or even notice it.

The water turned on again and I breathed a small sigh of relief when Gregory skulked into the bathroom.

"Should be a free day." Ethan shrugged into a shirt before climbing to the top bunk with his phone. "One day on, one day off. Tomorrow, we can explore the mansion and meet up with other people."

"And after that?" I pulled my hat down a little more and headed toward the door that led out of the portable. Maybe I'd just take a walk around the small domicile in the guise of securing our sleeping area. After lights out, I'd sneak in and take a quick shower by myself.

"Another trial. We're stuck together in a team now, so you bastards better not blow it."

I huffed. "You didn't seem too worried about your buddies in the last trial."

I barely saw him shrug as I turned the door handle. "I'm no one's caretaker. If people can't keep up, that's their problem."

"Where are you going?" Orin asked from the far corner, staring at me with his deep, solemn eyes.

"Just to…" I made a circle with my finger. "Just to make sure things are good. Go ahead and hit the hay. I won't be long."

An hour later, after I'd made a million laps around the portable, I finally snuck back in, my limbs sore and my eyes drooping. I was exhausted, mentally and physically. I needed a good sleep and to wake up from this terrible nightmare. What I wouldn't give to be back home, to be in my own bed and to hear the twins snoring on the floor below me.

Deep shadows pooled in the corners of the room and a small slice of light cut across the middle of the floor from the bathroom. Rhythmic, deep breathing indicated the guys were sound asleep, the mounds of bodies snuggled into the crappy lumpy mattresses.

I quietly grabbed the sweats and underwear I'd set out and slipped into the bathroom, closing the door behind me. A square area with four shower heads was stationed in the corner, the heads definitely too close together for comfort. Green tile stretched from the shower area to under a urinal, and two toilet stalls were tucked in behind that. One sink with ample counter space stretched away with a large mirror hanging over it.

Unable to help it, I curled my lip at the setup. I bet the ladies' dorms and bathrooms were nicer. Girls' stuff was always nicer. And we didn't pee on the floor.

The shower spray was hard and warm, pelting my skin and melting away all the stress and worry. I hoped my dad was taking my leaving okay, and that Buck hadn't stormed to the farm demanding my head.

Homesickness pinched my gut as I shut off the water, a quick clean all I could afford under the circumstances. I turned, reaching for a towel on the stand next to the shower, when the door swung open and a sleepy, puffy-eyed Pete trudged in.

I froze.

He froze, his gaze rooted to my chest.

"Boobs?" he said in a hasty release of breath. He jolted and his eyes flicked downward, but I was already moving.

I'd been caught out as a girl, and on my first damn day.

THE END.

ABOUT THE AUTHORS

K.F. Breene is a *USA Today* Bestselling and Top 10 Kindle All-Star author of paranormal romance, urban fantasy and fantasy novels. With two million books sold, when she's not penning stories about magic and what goes bump in the night, she's sipping wine and planning shenanigans. She lives in Northern California with her husband, two children and out of work treadmill.

Sign up for her newsletter to hear about the latest news and receive free bonus content.
www.kfbreene.com

Shannon is a lot of things, and most of these are true. She's an author, mom, rider of horses, farm girl, heathen, softie, badass, Canadian. Juxtaposition incarnate.

She is the USA Today Bestselling author of the The Rylee Adamson Novels, The Elemental Series, The Nevermore Trilogy, A Celtic Legacy series, and the Venom Trilogy. Please visit her website for more information on her novels.

To learn more about Shannon and her books, go to:
www.shannonmayer.com

39212605R00134

Printed in Poland
by Amazon Fulfillment
Poland Sp. z o.o., Wrocław